THE SCIENCE OF
HAPPILY
EVER AFTER

THE SCIENCE OF
HAPPILY
EVER AFTER

What *Really* Matters in the Quest for Enduring Love

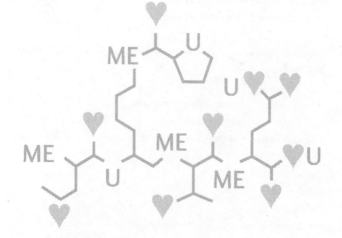

TY TASHIRO, Ph.D.

THE SCIENCE OF **HAPPILY** EVER AFTER

ISBN-13: 978-0-373-89290-7

Library of Congress Cataloging-in-Publication Data

Tashiro, Ty.

The science of happily ever after : what really matters in the quest for enduring love / Ty Tashiro, Ph.D.

pages cm

Includes bibliographical references and index.

ISBN 978-0-373-89290-7 (alk. paper)

1. Man-woman relationships. 2. Mate selection. 3. Love. 4. Interpersonal relations. I. Title.

HQ801.T276 2014

302.3--dc23

2013028710

To my mom and dad, for being happy
and loyal in every way imaginable.

CONTENTS

PART ONE

The Nature of Love

CHAPTER I

Why Happily Ever After Is So Hard to Find

I met Grant at a time in his life when he could not stop worrying. It would have been difficult to know from casual observation that Grant was beset by anxiety. Just a freshman, he was already revered by the engineering faculty for his ability to dismantle complicated scientific problems. His boyish looks, lanky build and crackling voice made his stunning intellect seem all the more precocious. Grant quickly made many new friends, who were endeared by his old-school politeness, good-natured temperament and even the occasions when he could be socially clumsy. However, when his mother passed away unexpectedly, the loss sent Grant into a state of constant anxiety. His high-powered brain spun his worries so rapidly and tightly that he found it difficult to move forward in his schoolwork and his social life. For some reason, the one thing that did not seem to worry him was the intern assigned to be his therapist: me.

I was beginning my second year of graduate school in psychology at the University of Minnesota, and Grant was one of my first clients. During our weekly meetings, Grant showed rapid progress as he dutifully followed the anxiety treatment protocols. For our sixth session, the protocol called for a public outing, and Grant suggested that we walk to a nearby coffee shop. We stepped outside into a blustering minus-ten-degree wind chill and pulled the hoods of our puffy coats tightly around our faces as Grant shared his good news.

Earlier in the week, while perusing old science books at a used bookstore, he saw an attractive young woman looking at old philosophy books in the same aisle. There are few social situations as anxiety provoking as trying to initiate a romantic encounter, and Grant's mental centrifuge started to spin. Before his anxieties could gain much momentum, she was walking toward him and asking about the book in his hand. They spent the next thirty minutes enthusiastically discussing philosophy and science. Grant was smitten. He was still describing the wonder that was Emma when he opened the door to the coffee shop, began walking inside and then suddenly stopped.

In one seamless motion, Grant whirled around, pushed me out the door and strained to whisper in his crackling voice, "Sir! She's in there!"

"Who's in there?"

"Emma! She must work here."

"Ah, jeez. What should we do?"

"I don't know! You're the psychologist."

"Right…"

We sat down on a bench to regroup. In the cold air, I could see Grant's breathing following a cadence of three breaths in, four breaths out, the same cadence I had taught him to employ when dealing with oncoming panic attacks. As Grant's anxiety rose, I took a deep breath, turned to him and put my hand on his shoulder in the most fatherly way I could imagine. Having no idea what a skilled therapist might instruct a client to do, I asked, *"You want to do this?"*

Grant thought for a brief moment, and then he stood up. He pursed his lips with determination, straightened his puffy coat and in his Minnesota accent said, "You betcha." We marched inside and stepped into line. As we waited, I peered around the group of fraternity pledges in front of us to get a look at this mysterious Emma. She was an edgy sort of lovely: a hipster with black cargo pants, a well-worn Ramones T-shirt and big brown eyes framed by Tina Fey–like glasses. She was moving efficiently, handling the high-maintenance orders and simultaneously engaging in casual banter with her customers.

When the pledges turned away from the register, the most handsome and well polished among them lingered at the counter to flirt with Emma. He looked like an NFL quarterback: tall, strong and confident. For some reason, this situation sparked a primal instinct within me, and I felt compelled to tackle him. Yet, I knew Grant needed to be the one to attack, to be at the counter right now and intervene. When I turned to Grant, he stood frozen.

With only the primitive fight-or-flight instincts of my hindbrain active, my reflexive thought was to kick Grant in the shin. So I did. Like a horse out of the chute, he burst toward the counter, and for a brief moment, I felt a sense of triumph. Here was Grant, charging forward with intent and momentum, on his way to winning Emma's heart, until he tripped. I gasped as he flew forward. When he finally landed, it was chest first on the edge of the counter. As Grant lay there in an awkward, angled plank position trying to regain his breath, the pledge, alarmed by the social awkwardness of the moment, shuffled to the end of the espresso bar.

As Grant lay on the counter, I wanted to pick him up and try to say something to break the awkward silence, but it was not my place.

I could only wait and watch. I felt like a coach standing helplessly on the sidelines, watching as his freshman kicker lined up to attempt a game-winning field goal.

What happened next was simply clutch. Grant looked up, gazed directly into Emma's bespectacled eyes and spoke in the timbre of an evening news anchor. "Emma, I'm Grant. We met at the bookstore the other day. I am captivated by the book you recommended. It is brilliant."

Emma blushed.

Grant made some witty jokes, and she laughed. She made some jokes, and he laughed.

At the end of it all, Emma suggested, "We should talk sometime, Grant... you know, about the book."

After the debacle and the brilliant recovery at the coffee shop, Grant and Emma went on three dates over the course of two weeks. All three dates were filled with engaging conversations, ample laughter and a rapidly increasing mutual attraction. However, Grant had not dated much in his lifetime and so how to proceed in a relationship was unfamiliar to him. In our therapy sessions, he asked dozens of questions about love, but the most significant of these was a question he asked me after their third date.

"I like Emma a lot."

"You do."

"I think I should kiss Emma."

"You should."

"Well, before that, I guess... Am I falling in love with Emma?"

"Maybe, Grant. But being in love... it's pretty complicated."

A LIFE IN LOVE

By the time I entered graduate school during the late 1990s, relationship science, the field devoted to the scientific study of relationships, was burgeoning after decades of researchers struggling against critics who argued that love was too complex to study or that love was a frivolous topic for scientific investigation. The University of Minnesota housed some of the best relationship researchers in the world, and under their guidance, I began to learn about the science of falling in love, staying in love and losing love.

My early research was focused on the endings of relationships—specifically, whether relationship breakups or divorce could lead to personal growth that might improve future relationships. In one of our first studies, Patricia Frazier and I asked ninety-two undergraduates experiencing a recent breakup to "describe what positive life changes, if any, have happened as a result of your breakup that might serve to improve your future romantic relationships." We found that the average participant reported five positive life changes, which included improved friendships, feeling more self-confident and learning how to better communicate. To our surprise, "will choose a better partner in the future" was one of the least cited types of growth.

Although supportive friends, self-confidence and communication skills contribute to healthy romantic relationships, a much stronger predictor of romantic success is the type of partner you choose in the first place. The traits that a partner possesses before you ever start dating, such as his or her personality and values, are among the strongest indicators of whether a romantic relationship will be happy and stable many years later. However, for people who say they will choose a better partner for the next relationship, the *intention* to choose a better partner does not guarantee that they will end up making better choices. How many times have you witnessed friends who are smart and effective people in most aspects of their lives repeatedly choose the same dysfunctional partners and then appear surprised when the relationship is a disaster a few months later?

Even if people do want to choose better partners, there is little sound guidance for this endeavor readily available from experts. For example, if I asked what you should do if you catch on fire or see a thief in your home, your response would be instantaneous. You would "stop, drop, and roll" to solve the first problem, and you would "call 9-1-1" to solve the second problem. Both responses are automatic and effective. Luckily, the chances of catching on fire are only .002 percent, and of encountering a robber just .004 percent. By comparison, the chances of divorcing in your lifetime (50 percent) are roughly twenty-five thousand times higher than the chances of catching on fire. So, it is unfortunate that there are few sound strategies readily available to singles who want to make wise decisions when it comes to choosing a partner.

This lack of a clear and effective strategy for choosing romantic partners was made apparent to me by Meagan, a precocious sophomore in my Interpersonal Relationships course at the University of Maryland. She wanted me to distill the vast academic research on mate selection into some practical advice that she could use in her love life. Her whimsical framing belied the incisive nature of the question. "Let's imagine you are single and looking for Mr. Right when a fairy godmother appears and grants one wish for your love life," she said to me. "What would be the best way to spend that wish so that you live happily ever after?"

Admittedly, my response sounded remarkably unscientific. "The best thing to wish for," I said, "would be a crystal ball."

I was perplexed by the mystical nature of my response, but upon more reflection later that day, on my metro ride home, I realized that the concept of a crystal ball is exactly what singles need before embarking on the long journey to happily ever after. Imagine how much heartache could be averted if you could look into a crystal ball after every first date. Instead of having to go through months of painful trial and error in the middle of the process, while trying to find out whether a partner would provide misery or happiness, with a crystal ball you would know from the beginning whether a partner was good for you or not.

Fortunately, advances in relationship science can make this wish for a crystal ball come true. Researchers are discovering how to predict what a relationship will be like years into the future by assessing the traits of the partners, such as personality, values and interests. Furthermore, these traits can be decoded in the early stages of dating, which can permit singles to predict with more accuracy which relationships will end up happily ever after.

However, the materials needed to construct this crystal ball are dispersed in a sea of thousands of scientific papers spanning a range of academic disciplines, including psychology, anthropology, demography and medical science. In the chapters to come, I will distill this mass of research literature into a manageable framework for choosing better partners and will put you on the path to a lifetime of love.

This is not a prescriptive self-help book promising a soul mate in three easy steps. Love is too complex and too personal for a stranger to tell a unique individual like you precisely what to do with your love life. Instead, my goal is to help you clarify your version of "happily ever after" and then to provide you with the information needed to make wise decisions when choosing a partner. To achieve this, we will answer the following questions in the chapters to come:

- What does "happily ever after" really mean, and why do only three in ten people find it?

- Why do we get only three wishes for an ideal partner, and why do most people wish for the wrong things?

- What three traits should you look for in a partner if you want to significantly improve the odds of finding enduring love?

The Science of Happily Ever After is about making smarter choices. It's about learning to weed out the undesirable traits and rethinking our views about what really matters in a romantic partner.

First, we need to take a closer look at the ultimate goal and determine what it really means to be happily in love and why being in love can become so complicated.

THE LANGUAGE OF LOVE

Like Grant, many people wonder what it means to be in love. Google has become an informal method for gauging what most people are searching for. Based on the most common searches, Google can anticipate what people might ask before they are done typing the full question. For example, "Am I in..." can be finished in dozens of ways, resulting in such questions as "Am I in trouble?" or "Am I in cahoots?" However, people are not primarily interested in their state of culpability or conspiracy, because when I typed the phrase "Am I in... ," the top five results were:

1. Am I in love?

2. Am I in labor?

3. Am I in love with him?

4. Am I insane?

5. Am I in love with him quiz?

For most of the five thousand years that marriage has existed, deciding whether you were in love with a partner did not matter, because until the eighteenth century marriage was primarily an economic agreement between families. Stephanie Coontz is an anthropological researcher at the Evergreen State College who studies the historical context of marriage, and she explains that the potential for sons and daughters to fall in love was rarely the primary criterion used by parents when choosing their children's partners. Decisions were more often based on how much livestock or land could be exchanged for a daughter's hand in marriage.

A good illustration of how pivotal being in love has become in many contemporary cultures comes from a study conducted by Robert Levine at California State University and his colleagues affiliated with universities in Japan and India. They wanted to know if the importance of being in love for major commitments, like marriage, is universal across cultures. Participants from eleven countries around the world were asked, "If a partner had *all* the characteristics that you wanted in a partner, but you were not in love with him/her, would you marry him/her?" While 49 percent of respondents from Pakistan and 48 percent from India answered yes, only 2.5 percent of respondents from the United States said they would marry someone with whom they were not in love, even if the person had everything else they desired in a mate.

If the key criterion for deciding whom to marry is being in love, then how do people know when they are in love? In addition to consulting Google, singles looking for some guidance about the meaning of love sometimes ask their engaged or married friends, "How did you know when you had found 'the one'?" The typical answer is usually less than satisfying. "You just know." This is like asking a chef who has crafted a wonderful meal behind closed doors, "How did you make this?" only to have her or him respond, "You just cook it." What singles are looking for is something more descriptive of how the experience develops. They want the ingredients and the steps for combining those ingredients to create the final product.

However, love is difficult to define. English, unlike some other languages, has just one word for *love*. As Ellen Berscheid summarized in a recent review of research about the meaning of love, there are many different situations, feelings and recipients associated with the concept of love. This confusion can make it difficult to think in precise ways about love and that ultimately makes it more difficult for us to find exactly what we are looking for. There is love associated with fellowship (companionate), support (compassionate) and sex (erotic), to name a few types, and there is love of family, friends, objects and sexual partners, to name a few possible recipients of our love.

Type of Love	Definition
Companionate	Friendship, togetherness
Compassionate	Caring, helping
Erotic	Lustful, sexual
Passionate	Strong physiological arousal, obsessive thought

One of the most useful definitions for the type of love most people want in a long-term romantic relationship came from the results of two studies conducted by Ellen Berscheid and her colleague Sarah Meyers. Previous research had investigated forms of love, such as companionate or erotic love, but Berscheid and Meyers wanted to see if people make a distinction between loving and being *in* love. The subtitle of their article, "The Difference That a Preposition Makes," alludes to their findings. In the first study, conducted with a sample of undergraduates, participants reported *loving* many things, including their friends, pets, brothers or girlfriends. However, when it came to being *in love,* the overwhelming majority of participants used this term only when referring to their romantic partners. There is, indeed, something awkward about saying that you are in love with your brother or your Chihuahua.

In a second study, Berscheid and Meyers recruited a new group of participants and provided them with dozens of terms (e.g., trust, intimacy, passion) and asked them to use as many of the terms needed to describe what it means to be in love. Out of dozens of possible descriptors, 86 percent of participants designated just two as the *essential* ingredients of being in love: liking and lust.

So, falling in love sounds simple, but requiring both liking and lust to be in love actually creates a very complex situation. Most relationship types can endure based on just one kind of love, such as friendships based on compassionate or companionate love, or purely sexual relationships, like "hookups" or "friends with benefits," which are narrowly based on erotic love. However, being *in love* with someone requires a complex mixture of love, one associated with liking (companionate, compassionate) and lust (erotic, passionate). Imagine how unhappy you would be with a romantic relationship if when asked about it, you replied, "It's great, except that I don't like hanging out with her...." or "It's great, except that I am physically repulsed by him...." Thus, when it comes to finding someone with whom we can fall in love, that someone is expected to provide the forms of love we use to describe our relationships with friends, pets, family and hookups.

While this romantic cornucopia confers more benefits, like most things in life, more goodness also means more maintenance. Once couples fall in love, there comes a day when one or both partners think about "taking it to the next level," which usually means doing something that will solidify their commitment to the relationship. Being in love often triggers important decisions, such as moving in together or getting married. If someone makes it past the checkpoints of finding a partner, dating and falling in love and all the way to the point of commitment, then he or she often reach the longest stretch of the road to happily ever after: marriage.

WHAT ARE THE ODDS OF FINDING HAPPILY EVER AFTER?

To demonstrate what happens to love over time, I aggregated the results of about a dozen well-conducted longitudinal studies of marriage. In these studies, researchers typically recruited dating couples or newlyweds and assessed the couples' satisfaction and functioning through multiple methods, including participants' self-reports of their marital functioning, coding videos of couples discussing problems in their relationship and physiological responses, such as heart rate. These assessments were repeated annually, and this gave researchers a window into what happened to marriage over the course of many years.

The good news is that the beginning of marriage is almost pure bliss. In one landmark study, conducted by Ted Huston and his colleagues at the University of Texas at Austin, it was found that couples in their first year of marriage scored in the eighty-sixth percentile on marital satisfaction. However, as the old saying goes, the honeymoon does not last. Dramatic declines in marital satisfaction occur in the second and third years of marriage. During the fourth and fifth years of marriage, couples can anticipate a less severe decline in satisfaction, before experiencing another large drop during years six and seven. By the end of the seventh year of marriage, couples on average score just below the fiftieth percentile on marital satisfaction and then experience a slow decline in satisfaction until about the twentieth year of marriage.

Furthermore, studies of divorce suggest that marital instability is the norm, not the exception. The divorce rate often reported by the media is 50 percent, which is based on Census Bureau data. However, census data does not capture the 10 to 15 percent of couples who permanently separate but do not file formal paperwork for a legal divorce.

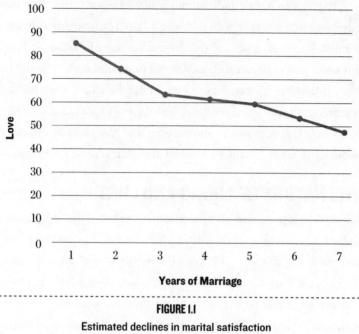

FIGURE I.I

Estimated declines in marital satisfaction
during the first seven years of marriage.

This means that a conservative estimate of the divorce and permanent separation rate is 60 percent. Add the additional 7 percent of chronically unhappy couples who do not divorce or permanently separate but are consistently unhappy in their marriage, and this means that two-thirds of all married couples *do not* live happily ever after.

Although this all sounds quite depressing, I prefer to look at the glass as one-third full. Instead of resigning ourselves to marital odds that are stacked against us, we should see if something might distinguish the 33 percent who find enduring love from the 67 percent who end up unhappy or unstable.

To give us a better understanding of why some people find happily ever after and others do not, we need to further dismantle what being in love means, study how the smaller parts function and then put these pieces back together with an improved understanding of what it takes to find enduring love. What we will see next is that researchers have discovered much about how liking emerges in childhood, how lust develops in adolescence and how this can inform us about what happens to liking and lust in adult romantic relationships.

THE NATURE OF LIKING AND LUST

Liking develops in early childhood and bears a striking resemblance to how adults evaluate their liking for others. Thomas Berndt is a professor of psychology at Purdue University who studies how liking develops, and in a summary of existing research he finds that children show strong similarities in the criteria they use to decide if they like someone. Friendships characterized by high degrees of liking are what researchers call "quality friendships," and they are characterized by three components: fairness, kindness and loyalty.

The first component of liking is *prosocial behavior,* which essentially means kind behavior. Kindness in friendships takes the form of providing praise after successes, and moral support after failures, and generously giving to friends with no immediate expectation of payback. In adult romantic relationships, kindness takes the form of showing support and enthusiasm when partners tell us about their successes, and steadfast emotional support when they share their difficulties and struggles.

If we are kind to others, then we need a sense that this giving will be reciprocated. The second component of liking is *fairness,* and in childhood this often translates as "I'll do this for you if you do this for me" and manifests as sharing or turn taking. Although this expectation of equal exchange becomes less rigid as we get older, adults continue to be good accountants of relationship events. Even in communal relationships, in which giving is not seen as a one for one exchange of goods or favors, people generally trust that their giving will be reciprocated by their partners.

Loyalty is the third component of liking and goes hand in hand with the idea that others can be relied upon to be steadfast and trustworthy. Loyalty becomes increasingly important as we enter adolescence and adulthood, and in adult romantic relationships, loyalty is at the core of traditional marital vows, "...for better, for worse, in sickness and in health, for richer, for poorer, until death do us part."

Most kids and adults figure out how to form relationships characterized by mutual liking and are able to sustain those relationships for many years. In fact, most kids have at least a core group of three or four friends who are more often than not kind, fair and loyal. It can be emotional to watch childhood friendships function well, because it all seems so perfect. Parents will sometimes say that they wish that time could stop and life for their children could stay like that forever. Of course, time does not stop, and eventually kids become adolescents.

Around twelve to thirteen years of age, dramatic physical changes take place that make adolescents capable of sexual activity and reproduction, including sperm production for boys and ovulation for girls. These physical changes coincide with the psychological onset of lust, which is defined as a state of sexual desire. Although boys and girls both experience increases in lust during adolescence, *what* they desire tends to be very different, and these qualitative differences persist into adulthood.

Leticia Peplau, a pioneering social psychologist from UCLA who studies human sexuality, has focused part of her research on how men and women lust differently. One way to study lust is to ask research participants about their sexual fantasies, and in a review of gender differences in lust, Peplau found that boys fantasize 33 percent more often than girls do. The content of their fantasies differs, as well. Boys' sexual fantasies are typically envisioned through a zoomed lens perspective on the mechanics of sex. Boys fantasize about many different sexual partners, and they often fantasize about partners they do not know well and even complete strangers. Girls tend to take a panoramic perspective, envisioning romantic scenes or meaningful conversation as a context for being physically intimate. Compared to boys, girls are twice as likely to fantasize about sexual partners they know well. In other words, girls tend to lust for partners they also like.

When being in love is broken into its smaller parts, we see that it is three parts liking to one part lust.

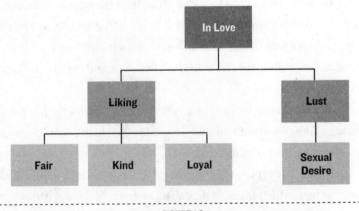

FIGURE I.2

Components of being "In Love" from descriptive studies of love.

Liking is composed of ingredients such as loyalty and unconditional giving, which help people ensure the longevity of their familial relationships and friendships. Lust, on the other hand, stems from biological urges, which, we will see, are far more mercurial.

WHAT HAPPENS TO LIKING AND LUST IN ROMANTIC RELATIONSHIPS?

For the purpose of the following thought experiment, let's assume that there are equal amounts of liking and lust at the beginning of a marriage. In the graph below are the results from a fourteen-year longitudinal study of marriage by Ted Huston and his colleagues at the University of Texas at Austin. Couples in this study were enrolled before they were married, were tracked intensively as they made the transition to marriage, and then were assessed every few years on variables that included liking, passionate love and divorce. Liking declines at a rate of 3 percent a year, whereas lust declines at a rate of 8 percent per year.

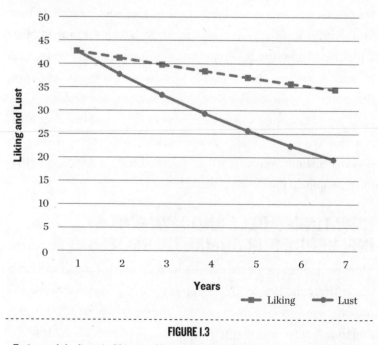

FIGURE 1.3
Estimated declines in liking and lust during the first seven years of marriage.

According to the studies of liking, the components of liking (such as fairness and loyalty) are intended to help relationships endure over time. In contrast, lust stems from biological and psychological urges that motivate people primarily toward mating. In other words, lust is helpful for encouraging people to procreate, but less useful when it comes to sustaining a sense of happiness in a long-term relationship, because lust depreciates at a much faster rate than liking. If one is looking to stay in love for a long time, then investing disproportionately in liking over lust seems to be the smart investment strategy.

Sometimes I am asked why infatuation and the feelings that accompany it, such as butterflies in the stomach or a racing heart, cannot last. These visceral feelings are powerful feelings of lust, and they cannot last for a simple reason: you would die. Butterflies in the stomach are the result of a surge of endorphins, but this also triggers the release of hormones, such as cortisol, that become toxic to your brain with years of chronic exposure. Another term for a racing heart is high blood pressure. So, even though the lust component of being in love drives a very intense and visceral type of emotional experience, the intensity of passionate love is necessarily ephemeral.

Given our review of what happens to liking and lust over time, it seems that a completely rational person would invest disproportionately in liking versus lust from the start. So why is it the case that most people do the exact opposite?

HOW TINKER BELL AND *TWILIGHT* INFLUENCE OUR ROMANTIC BELIEFS

Most people yearn for passionate love that lasts forever, which is not entirely the fault of the hopeless romantic. As we will see, the messages we receive from our environments about what love is and how it is found are often irrational and unhelpful. Our social environments—which include our parents, friends and the mass media, to name a few sources—provide a narrative or a "how-to" about how we should fall in love. These messages strongly shape our beliefs about what love should be and about the partners we choose to love.

What are the environments that surround children and adolescents the most? In a recent survey of time use, researchers for Kaiser hospitals asked more than ten thousand eight- to eighteen-year-olds how they spend their time. What they found was that young people now spend most of their time—7.5 hours a day, or 45 percent of their waking hours—interacting with their computers, phones, tablets and other electronic devices. Much of their time on these devices is spent interacting with mass media, such as television, the internet or gaming. By comparison, they are in school 30 percent of the time, they spend 20 percent of their time engaged in leisure activities with friends, and they spend only 10 percent of the day with their parents.

Mass media exposure is not a passive process. Young people actively seek out mass media, not just as a source of entertainment but also as a form of guidance, and that includes direction regarding their love lives. When communications studies professor Christine Bachen from the University of Santa Barbara and sociologist Eva Illouz from the University of Tel Aviv interviewed 183 children aged seven to seventeen about which sources they look to for romantic advice, they found that 90 percent of these children reported looking to television shows and movies. Other seemingly good sources of advice lagged far behind, such as participants' mothers (33 percent) and fathers (17 percent). In another study, Bjarne Holmes and Kimberly Johnson of Heriot-Watt University investigated whether the amount of television consumed by young adults in romantic relationships was associated with more irrational beliefs about relationships, including men and women being destined to have gender-based conflicts and the partner being able to read the other's mind. Importantly, consuming more television was also linked with less relationship satisfaction in the subjects' actual romantic relationships.

Children's Fairy-Tale Beliefs about Love

Children develop their beliefs about romance by observing their parents' interactions, from watching movies, and even from listening to stories read to them at bedtime. Early literary analysts, such as the Russian scholar Vladimir Propp, analyzed the content of dozens of fairy tales to look for consistent themes across stories. What he and others have found is that there is remarkable consistency in the characters and plots across fairy tales.

There is usually a heroic prince who longs for a beautiful girl, and a girl who will love him for his true self and not his public facade. Meanwhile, the beautiful girl is caged by oppressive circumstances and waits for a strong, brave hero to free her. It would surely be love at first sight, but evil forces conspire to keep both of them from seeing the love that could be. At the climax, when it seems as if evil will triumph and love will never be found, the swift hand of fate intervenes. Magic wands swish. Spells are cast. Glitter is thrown. Suddenly, rags are turned into ball gowns, or frogs are transformed into princes. It is love at first sight, the prince and princess marry, and everyone "...lives happily ever after." Given the assurance that all is well, children doze off and enter a dreamland filled with magical tales of falling in love.

Consistent with literary analysts' observations of fairy-tale themes, Litsa Tanner and her colleagues examined the romantic beliefs in popular Disney films and coded twenty-six Disney films for recurring themes related to couples or families. What they found is that most of the films depict protagonists falling in love within minutes, portray physical beauty as an "ideal" and end with the couple "living happily ever after." So it is not surprising that when you ask children what they wish for in love, many can provide elaborate descriptions of future marital partners who will be beautiful, brilliant and brave. If you ask them what will happen when they find this dreamy partner, they shoot you that incredulous look reserved for grown-ups who should know better. When it comes to the person you plan to love forever, why would you do anything else but live happily ever after?

Adolescents' Tragic Beliefs about Love

While children drift into dreams of finding love, teenagers awaken to the hormonal eruption propelling them to fall *in* love. In their English classes, adolescents read romantic tragedies, such as *Romeo and Juliet,* which are tales of star-crossed lovers. The protagonists are fated to love each other, but love blinds them to rational judgment, and thus they meet a tragic end. When teens go home, they read modern tragedies, such as the novels in the *Twlight* series, which are tales of an ordinary teenage girl who sees her soul mate through the pouring rain, his silhouette illuminated by the faint glow of twilight. This beautiful boy is emotionally unavailable, abhors sunshine and wants to suck her blood until she is soulless. Alas, she cannot help loving him; her love is fated.

In romantic tragedies, it matters little whether the prince is a Montague or a Cullen, the beautiful girl a Capulet or a Swan. The embedded romantic beliefs are timeless. Similar to childhood fairy tales, love just happens when fate delivers a soul mate. However, these fated romances do not end in happily ever after. Adolescents fall in love so quickly and deeply, not realizing that the speed at which two people fall in love and the emotional weight of committing to another person multiply the force with which people can fall flat on their faces. The problem begins with the belief in a "one and only."

If there is only one fated love, then what happens if the romance is ill-fated? This often means enduring a tragic life with the one and only until the bitter end. When adolescents lose their one and only love, it can seem as if a love like that will never be found again. Not now. Not ever.

One common message in childhood fairy tales and in adolescenet romantic tragedies is the notion that fate is responsible for people falling in love. However, these messages of fated love, suggesting that love "just happens" or that people magically "live happily ever after," are not only quixotic but also counterproductive. One of the problems in modern romance is that trusting in fate leads people to look for love in the wrong places and instills false beliefs about how love endures. It is easy to forget that the message in most fairy tales is that people usually wish for the wrong things, and many adolescents find out the hard way that someone sucking on your neck does not make your love immortal. It gives you a hickey. Looking for fate or a mystical force to deliver enduring love is a losing proposition.

A GROWN-UP LOVE STORY

Unfortunately, the romantic beliefs of fated love and "one and only" soul mates do not end in childhood or adolescence. In a 2010 Gallup survey of more than one thousand adults, respondents were asked if they believed that there is a soul mate, which most people define as a "one and only" partner whom they are fated to be with forever and who is waiting for them. The overwhelming majority (88 percent) said yes. Although there is nothing wrong with believing that a spiritual connection in love can be *worked* toward, counting on fate to magically provide the right partner and a relationship high in satisfaction and stability is a shot in the dark.

Believing that love should be left to fate and then committing to love someone forever based upon fairy-tale beliefs, rather than willfully choosing partners with the traits needed for enduring love, is a mind-set that likely contributes to only three in ten couples finding enduring love. A grown-up love story should not be a fairy tale or a romantic tragedy, but instead should be approached as a mystery. If the goal is to find the truth in love, to search for love that is real and enduring, then love cannot be left to fate. Mysteries always begin with a crime and with investigators searching for who or what is responsible for the crime. Investigators search for concrete clues, organize those clues into plausible theories, and then solve the mystery through a bit of reason and intuition.

In this chapter, we have arrived at the scene of the crime to find a dismal marital scene. Although 90 percent of people will marry in their lifetime, only three in ten will find enduring love. However, we have begun to unravel why so many relationships fail. We have seen that falling out of love has something to do with lust declining at a faster rate than liking. We also know that the traits of potential partners provide additional clues as to why so few people find happily ever after. In the next chapter we turn to thinking about how to choose a better partner and examining why you get only three wishes for love.

In the end, there are few things in life so worthwhile of careful study and judicious decision making as whom to love. For there are few things in life so demoralizing as the disappointment accompanying a broken heart, and conversely, there are few things so elevating as finding love that endures.

THE CLUES ABOUT HAPPILY EVER AFTER ARE FOUND IN YOUR PARTNER

One evening during the summer of 2008, I arrived at Washington National Airport after a long work trip. I had been meeting with coauthors to put the finishing touches on a chapter about the consequences of divorce, a process that had not left me feeling optimistic about love. As I waited at the baggage carousel, I felt a hand firmly grasp my shoulder, and I turned around to see Grant and his fiancée, Emma.

My mind flashed back to the coffee shop seven years earlier. It had struck me that most people would have thought Grant a fool after he tripped so spectacularly onto the counter. Yet Emma reserved passing judgment on Grant and instead remained perfectly calm, perhaps anticipating that Grant would be mortified and that her being reactive would make him feel even worse. Emma's grace under awkwardness allowed Grant, who had been fraught with anxiety, to proceed without fear. Many of her behaviors allowed me to form early hypotheses about her traits. When he complimented her, she was modest. When she asked him out, she was confident. Perhaps most importantly, Emma's sense of security in herself gave Grant a fluidity, a range that allowed him to be his best possible self. When a partner enables this kind of comfortable range, it is a promising sign that enduring love might be possible.

Minnesotans will tell you there are some winter nights when the harsh southeast winds, which can be so piercingly cold and utterly disorienting, will suddenly subside. The still air brings about a peaceful silence, and the moonlight seems more luminous. During the winter of 2001, at the end of their third date, Grant and Emma stood face-to-face on her porch on one such night. They maintained the customary eighteen inches of personal space, talking about how much fun they had together, and then there was an audible silence —the kind of pause that occurs when people are preoccupied with what should be happening in a given situation. Gazing into Emma's eyes, Grant ever so slowly began to lean into her space.

In our meeting earlier that week, we had discussed his desire to kiss Emma and whether he was in love with her. Before he left that day, he vented one last doubt before opening the door. He feared that becoming romantically involved with Emma could put at risk the companionship of someone so kind, trusting and loyal. When he finished saying the words aloud, he looked at me, grinned with relief and knowingly nodded his head.

So I was not surprised to learn what happened on Grant and Emma's date when they stood face-to-face, gazing into each other's eyes, during that luminous winter night. As Grant inched forward into Emma's personal space, she clutched the lapels of his jacket, drew him close and kissed him.

CHAPTER 2

Why You Get Three Wishes for Love (And No More)

On Christmas Eve, during her senior year of high school, my friend Anna decided to have sex for the first time. Unlike most aspects of her life, she had no particular reason for waiting until her senior year of high school to have sex. She had been too busy to think of such silly things. She maintained a perfect grade point average, was a volleyball star and taught Sunday school at St. Vincent's Catholic Church.

Her sharp German features, strong shoulders and severe bangs were intensely attractive in an "I must break you" kind of way. I have never been the masochistic type, and Anna was never fond of watching human train wrecks up close—a mismatch of preferences that made us perfectly platonic friends. Anna was able to appreciate my strengths in the domain of leisure, one of the few things that did not come naturally to her. So, when she needed a break from being awesome at life, she would come find me in the library—where I spent my first period in a study block, which preceded my second period PE class—and drive me downtown for a dozen doughnuts at the Winchell's on old Main Street.

Without the pressures of her parents, teachers and coaches, Anna was a delight. Her wall of expectations and her anxiousness to please others would melt away, freeing her best self. As we discussed the important matters of high school life, she would transform from someone best described as intense into someone interesting. For Anna to accomplish this window of contentment simply required a dozen doughnuts, a pint of chocolate milk and an underachieving friend.

One December morning, Anna told me about something she needed to "take care of." Anna maintained a series of lists on oversize yellow legal pads, which afforded her the space necessary to accommodate her ambitions. Anna pulled out one of her lists. For some reason, having sex for the first time had risen to Roman Numeral I, Part A.

"I've decided it's time to have sex."

"Well, then, do you have a special—"

"Of course not. But I need to do it. I'm eighteen years old. I'm a senior."

"Well, what type of guy do you want to—"

"Three things. Hot, athletic and Catholic."

In hindsight, there were many perplexing elements to our conversation. However, at the time, I was nonplussed maybe because I assumed Anna had already thought this decision through on a legal pad. After scouring the landscape of five hundred available men at Skyline High School, we came up with a short list of five candidates, whom Anna underlined with the palpable intent of someone brimming with sexual frustration.

One boy clearly embodied the three characteristics better than any of the other candidates. Jake was a fifteen-year-old man-child, best known for assuming the starting quarterback position through a mixture of stunning athleticism and sheer size. He was an Adonis-like 185 pounds of muscle packed onto a six-two frame. As a fringe benefit to the athleticism and hotness, Anna also liked the way his tan forearms rippled when he gripped the football. To cap it all off, his family attended St. Vincent's Catholic Church.

In the days that followed our meeting, Anna executed her action items with remarkable efficiency. She became a greeter at church and began to extend her weight-lifting time to overlap with the football team's lifting time. Fourteen days after our discussion, Anna reported that she and Jake had French-kissed in the parking lot of a local pizza joint. In a methodical fashion, Anna decided that they would progress to second base on the second date, third base on the third date. For their fourth date, which was scheduled to occur after Christmas Eve Mass, Jake and Anna planned to exchange gifts, and unbeknownst to Jake, Anna knew that this would be the night that they would have sex for the first time.

On Christmas Eve, the congregation concluded the evening Mass by walking outdoors while holding small white candles and singing "Silent Night." Anna wore a silky egg-shell white dress. While the congregation lifted their voices to the starry heavens, she subtly looked to the left and gazed at Jake's cherubic face and his forearms, which were somehow rippling through the sleeves of his white wool sweater. Marveling at Jake's beauty, strength and breathy rendition of "Silent Night," Anna found herself overwhelmed with lust.

After Mass, Anna's parents were going to a holiday party, leaving her house empty for a couple of hours. Jake and Anna drove to Anna's home in silence, the heated air thick with anticipation. When they arrived, Anna led Jake down the long staircase to the basement. She turned on a pair of silver-plated reindeer lamps, the twelve original bulbs replaced with alternating green and red bulbs by her mother.

They sat down on the cushy white carpet and exchanged gifts, which included a pair of red socks with a Santa Claus sewn on each side from Anna to Jake. She demonstrated for Jake that pushing Santa's nose started a tinny rendition of "Silver Bells."

Jake took off his penny loafers and black socks and pulled up each of the red Santa socks to his knees. When Jake looked toward Anna to share his amusement, she mounted him. Within seconds, white clothing was flying around the basement. After a few more seconds, they were totally naked. Except for Jake's Santa socks, which were too snug on his muscular calves and too much effort to remove given the task to be accomplished. It was the fourth date. It was time. So, with "Silver Bells" playing in rounds as mood music, Anna and Jake consummated this highly anticipated sexual encounter.

The sex was... brief.

When Jake collapsed in Anna's arms, he declared with exasperated relief, "I did it!" Anna's tactile senses quickly subsided, allowing other senses to click on in rapid succession. The tinny sounds of "Silver Bells" swirled around her ears, her eyes narrowed toward the saliva-soaked Communion bread lodged in Jake's braces, and her brow furrowed as the bitter taste of reality overcame her. In their haste, they had forgotten to use any form of contraception.

What if she had just procreated with, of all people, Jake?

Anna called me on Christmas morning, and for the first time during our three years of friendship, she sounded scared. I suppose it was the first time in Anna's life that her future seemed uncertain. She contemplated what seemed like a long and miserable future. "What if Jake never figures out how to read blitzes and no college programs want to recruit him? What if he cannot pass English lit to graduate? What if he talks incessantly about football every Sunday of every fall for the rest of our lives?"

She could bear the thought of a child, but she could not bear the thought of a lifetime of Sundays with Jake. Anna wondered aloud so many times during those uncertain days, "Why did I choose that guy?"

HOW DO PEOPLE SELECT ROMANTIC PARTNERS?

In the studies I have conducted on couples, I have been surprised by how many partners in unhappy relationships have difficulty recalling what first attracted them to their current partner. In one study published in the Journal of Counseling Psychology in 2007, Patricia Frazier and I recruited forty-seven dating couples to come into the lab for a study of emotion and problem solving. Part of the experimental manipulation involved a plan to rouse positive emotions by asking couples to take five minutes to answer the question, "What initially attracted you to your partner?" We were stunned by how difficult this task was for many couples. Pure bewilderment overcame some of them, which created a deafening silence as they sat face-to-face for five excruciating minutes. As one participant put it, "You wake up one day and wonder how you could have possibly been attracted to this person and stayed together for so long."

Relationships are so complex and emotionally distracting that it can be easy to forget how love comes about in the first place, and before you know it, you have been dating for two years or have been married for twenty. Taking a step back to consider how relationships begin in the first place can be helpful for understanding how people like Anna choose "that guy."

Relationships begin when two people meet for the first time, become attracted to one another and then try to make a relationship work. How two people combine in a relationship is well illustrated by a principle many of us learned in elementary school.

When I was in third grade, I received an assignment in art class to make a painting of my house using watercolors. After painting the brownstone house where I lived, I wanted to paint the aspen trees that lined its perimeter. To my chagrin, I found the green oval was missing from my watercolor tray. Thinking that all was lost and that a house without green trees was no house at all, I buried my bowl-cut head of hair in my small hands. My art teacher, seeing the young artist's angst, walked to my table, knelt down and gently asked to borrow my paintbrush.

She dipped my brush in a bit of yellow paint and dabbed some of the yellow on a piece of scratch paper. She then took some blue paint and began to mix it with the yellow paint. As I watched the color green appear, it seemed magical to me. Of course, it was not magic, but rather a demonstration of a fundamental scientific principle: some things manifest themselves only after two distinct elements are combined.

Similarly, it is hard to know what a relationship will look like until two people combine and settle into it. Two people coming together in a romantic relationship is not simply additive; relationships are a unique product of each person's traits, which combine to form something new. So when two people first meet, it can be difficult to imagine what will happen. By analogy, all you can see at first is that you are yellow and your new partner is blue.

This process of two people combining in a relationship is well depicted in a visual representation of closeness from social psychologist Art Aron and his colleagues. Hoping to develop a single visual measure of how close people feel to each other, Aron and his colleagues present couples with two circles that range from non-overlapping to almost entirely overlapping. When couples indicate higher degrees of overlap, this is associated with self-reports of relationship intimacy, closeness, and with whether dating couples are still together three months later.

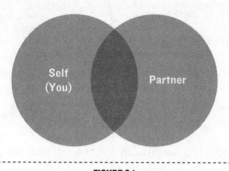

FIGURE 2.1

Interdependence between the Self and Partner.

The degree of overlap between the two circles represents the amount of closeness the Self (you) and a Partner (the other person) have in a relationship. Researchers often depict the intersection of the circles as "Self X Partner," instead of "Self + Partner," which is a helpful way of showing that a relationship is a unique product of the Self's and the Partner's distinct traits interacting. This S X P does not depict closeness in relationships as the Self and the Partner losing themselves by being in the relationship, but rather it demonstrates that becoming close can create new possibilities when the Self and the Partner interact. For example, imagine a couple in which the Self is very creative and the Partner is very conscientious. If they can work together collaboratively, then they can probably accomplish much more through the interaction of their unique traits in the relationship.

The qualities that are inherent or characteristic of the Self and the Partner are what psychologists call traits. Some examples of commonly considered traits in romantic partners can span categories such as physical qualities, abilities and personality. Traits describe what is consistent, and therefore relatively predictable, about a given person.

Physical Traits	Abilities	Personality
Facial Attractiveness	Intelligence	Novelty Seeking
Bodily Attractiveness	Athleticism	Kindness
Gender	Earning Potential	Extroversion
Race	Sense of Humor	Conscientiousness

Well-conducted longitudinal studies that track people from childhood through older adulthood strongly suggest that traits do not change much across the life span. Extroverted children tend to grow up to be extroverted adults, and thrill-seeking teens become ornery retirees. One of the biggest mistakes is to hope that a partner will make wholesale changes to their traits or, even worse, that getting married or having a child will dramatically change the traits of a partner. The traits a partner possesses during the first couple years of dating are indicative of how the partner will behave as your roommate, your financial partner, your friend and a parent. The stability of traits can be good news or bad news depending on what kind of traits you chose in the first place.

However, accurately reading a partner's traits can be difficult at the beginning of a relationship, because when two people first start to become close, the unique chemistry is so exhilarating. The infatuation early in relationships often creates overly rosy perceptions of the partner's traits and the relationship's characteristics, which is a phenomenon social psychologists Sandra Murray and John Holmes call "positive illusions."

In a review of forty-eight studies of positive illusions in relationships, Garth Fletcher and Patrick Kerr from the University of Canterbury averaged the effects of these studies to investigate whether the inflated judgments of romantic partners occurred consistently across most studies. What they found is that the participants rated their partners' personalities, their partners' behaviors in the past and the chances of their relationship being satisfying in the future as significantly better than did outside judges, such as friends, family or researchers. This internal tendency to inflate our views of our partners is further complicated by another phenomenon: Murray and Holmes have found that partners consistently engage in "strategic self-presentation" by putting their best traits on display while concealing their negative traits.

So, at the start of relationships, there are a number of factors working against your ability to make sound, accurate judgments about the partner and the relationship. Physiologically, we are racing with endorphins; psychologically, we are under the spell of positive illusions; and our partners are on their best behavior during the first few months of a relationship. This makes positive traits the easiest to see, but as the Self and the Partner become closer, previously unseen characteristics become more evident.

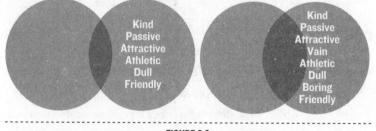

FIGURE 2.2
Some traits are revealed only when closeness increases.

The popular notion that people become intoxicated by love is not too far off base when considering the research about how impaired our judgment becomes. When you step away from it all, the thought of trying to drive through this state of infatuation to a more reasonable place seems like a bad idea. It would seem wise to hand off the keys to someone with more lucidity until your better sensibilities return, but for better or for worse, only you can drive yourself through the thick haze of infatuation.

Years can pass before the fog of infatuation dissipates, strategic self-presentation fades and the discordant tones of conflict begin to fully appear in a relationship. Before people realize who their partners are, they may have made commitments to relationships that make dissolving them more difficult. Moving in together, adopting a dog and getting married are all commitments that increase the barriers to breaking up, even if those relationships have become unsatisfying. When faced with the difficult task of breaking apart a failing relationship, in which so much time, energy and hope have been invested, people lament that they never saw the disastrous future sooner.

However, the seeds of relationship disaster can be seen early in the process of dating if you know how to spot certain traits that predict future relationship outcomes.

THE TRAITS OF YOUR IDEAL PARTNER

My friend Anna, like most people, wanted a certain "type" of partner who exhibited specific "traits." This notion can be heard in discussions of dating life. For instance, people say, "He's totally my type," or "She's got my look," which indicates preferences for certain traits. In Anna's case, she wanted three traits: hot, athletic and Catholic.

Traits improve our ability to predict someone's future behavior. For example, college football scouts would try to assess Jake's athleticism by evaluating his speed, strength and performance in games, in an attempt to determine whether Jake possessed the athletic traits that predict being a good collegiate football player. Likewise, psychologists are able to predict many important outcomes years later, things like life satisfaction, job performance, criminality and marital quality, because they know that people with certain traits will respond consistently across situations.

Informal discussions about traits as they relate to dating are frequently conducted among friends when they talk about someone's new love interest. These discussions usually begin with, "What is he like?" or "What is she like?"Although there are some people we meet who seem to defy explanation, we can usually rattle off a series of traits when describing a disastrous date or newfound love interest. I like to think that I do not possess the trait of being "nosy," but I must admit that I have overheard a discussion or two along the lines of this one:

Woman A: "So, what's he like?"

Woman B: "Well, he's a lawyer, and he studied at Georgetown. He's not that tall, but I think he works out. He has a nice body, and his eyes! He was really sweet, kind of talked a lot, but whatever. Anyways, I think that he is..."

She kept going, as most of us do when we are excited about telling someone else about a new partner, and the language we use to do that involves listing traits, such as the person's occupation ("lawyer"), intelligence (implied by dropping "Georgetown") and physical characteristics ("tall"). In this conversation, you can also hear in real time how woman B does not want "kind of talked a lot" to be interpreted as an indicator of negative traits, such as "self-centered" or "obnoxious." So, it is quite natural for us to categorize people's behavior into traits, because we have an intuitive sense that those traits can help us anticipate how they might respond to us or respond to situations in general.

In the table below, I created a list of traits commonly mentioned in studies that ask participants about what they desire in a romantic partner. In this brief exercise, circle those traits that you would want in an ideal partner. Do you want someone five-six or six feet tall? Average looking or very attractive?

What You Would Want in an Ideal Partner?

Height	5'4"	5'6"	5'8"	5'10"	6'0"	6'2"	6'4"
Income	$17,499	$24,999	$34,999	$59,999	$87,499	$99,999	> $149,000
Education	High School	Bachelors	Ph.D.		Doctor	Lawyer	
Politics	Republican	Democrat					
Religion	Catholic	Protestant	Jewish	Muslim	Buddhist	Agnostic/ Atheist	Other
Race	White	Latino	Black	Asian	Other		
Facial Attractiveness	Average	Attractive	Very Attractive				
Kind	Slightly Mean	Slightly Kind	Moderately Kind	Extremely Kind			
Exciting	Slightly Boring	Slightly Exciting	Moderately Exciting	Extremely Exciting			
Intelligence	Dull	Average	Bright	Very Bright			

Why You Get Three Wishes

There are two key questions to consider when developing a smart strategy for selecting a good partner. First, how much can you reasonably wish for in a partner? And second, how should those wishes be spent? What Anna had right about partner selection was to wish for three traits. However, the way in which Anna spent her wishes is where the partner selection process went awry. We will focus on how to spend wishes in subsequent chapters, but it is important to begin by examining why you get three wishes.

Imagine that someone wants a man who is "tall," and defines tall as someone six feet tall or taller. Only 20 percent of men are six feet tall or taller, which means that if you had a room of one hundred randomly selected bachelors and wanted only those six feet tall or taller, then eighty of the bachelors would have to leave the room. In fact, any choice outside the average range will severely limit your options. This does not imply an anticlimactic end to your love story, in which you are destined to grind out years with someone you find to be an average human being. Rather, it implies that you have to be very thoughtful about which traits you want that are above average in order to select someone with traits that are critical to finding happily ever after.

Percentage of Those Who Meet Each Criterion

Minimum Height (Men)	5'9" 50%	5'10" 40%	5'11" 30%	6'0" 20%	6'1" 10%	6'2" < 5%
Minimum Height (Women)	5'4" 50%	5'5" 40%	5'6" 20%	5'7" 10%	5'8" < 5%	
Annual Income	$35,000 50%	$45,000 40%	$60,000 30%	$87,000 20%	$100,000 10%	$150,000 < 5%
Education	High School 50%	Bachelors 30%	Ph.D. < 5%	Doctor < 5%	Lawyer < 5%	
Political Affiliation	Republican 27%	Democrat 31%	Independent 40%			
Religious Affiliation	Catholic 24%	Protestant 40%	Jewish < 5%	Muslim < 5%	Buddhist < 5%	Other < 5%
Race	White 62%	Latino 13%	Black 12%	Asian 4%	Other 9%	
Facial Attractiveness	Average 50%	Attractive 10%	Very Attractive < 5%			
Kind Personality	Slightly 50%	Moderately 20%	Extremely < 5%			
Exciting Personality	Slightly 50%	Moderately 20%	Extremely < 5%			
Intelligence	Average 50%	Bright 14%	Very Bright < 5%			

When Anna and I sat down in the library to figure out which boys were hot, athletic and Catholic, we began with a population of five hundred boys who attended our high school.[1] Her three wishes quickly whittled down the number of partners available:

---

[1] This simplified example does not take into account at least three factors that are always in play during Partner Selection: (1) 3 to 6 percent of those boys are attracted to other boys, (2) 30 percent of those high school boys are already in relationships, and (3) it is unknown how many of the remaining heterosexual, single boys would be mutually attracted to Anna as a romantic partner.

- Someone "hot" is probably in the top tenth percentile of physical attractiveness, which means only fifty of the five hundred boys would meet this criterion.

- Twenty-four percent of the population is Catholic, reducing the available boys from fifty to twelve.

- Only 10 percent of the boys started on a varsity sports team, reducing the number of boys available from twelve to 1.2.

- The mathematical product of Anna's three wishes was Jake.

I wish that everyone could get everything they want in one magical partner. However, if Anna added a fourth wish, let's say someone who identified with the Republican Party, it would have been mathematically improbable for her to find even one partner out of a pool of five hundred potential partners. Life would be much easier if we had unlimited wishes, but researchers examining what happens when people wish for too many things in a partner have found just how costly a "shopping spree for traits" approach can be.

I formulated a more informed answer about why Anna's field of options narrowed so quickly when I arrived at the University of Minnesota. I read a paper during my fifth year of graduate school that was written by two of the professors in our department, Auke Tellegen and David Lykken, in which they used a large database to investigate whether partner selection showed predictable patterns of purposeful choice. If people approach mate selection in a purposeful manner, then the data should show a certain pattern of some traits being more valued than others. Their findings across four different studies are well summarized by the title of the research report, "Human Mating Is Adventitious," which is to say that singles generally ended up selecting their partners by chance rather than by intent.

I found it fascinating that for all the time singles spend ruminating about their ideal partner, most probably do not end up getting many of the traits they envisioned. The Lykken and Tellegen research article, published in 1993, was one of the first studies to raise significant doubts about singles' ability to ultimately marry the kinds of partners they hoped for. The paper generated surprisingly less follow-up research by other scientists than I would have expected, which left me to sit down with my pen, paper and calculator. My curiosity piqued, I explored the following question, "How does this occur, that is, how do so many people not find what they are looking for?"

It seemed to me that one of the plausible explanations for the haphazard nature of the partner selection process was singles wishing for an unreasonable number of traits, such that it became mathematically improbable that they would get most of the traits they wanted. I found this to be a fascinating notion. It was a big problem to tackle, and so I set it aside while I continued pursuing my research on breakups and emotion in relationships. Yet I could not shake the idea, and my curiosity about why people ultimately don't get what they want in a romantic partner continued to grow, until it became so unwieldy that I had to sit down and write this book about why people get three wishes for love.

While I was scribbling down traits and probabilities in Minneapolis, I did not know that around the same time a Ph.D. student in physics at Harvard University was contemplating the same question. David Kestenbaum found his inspiration for the question not from a research article, but rather from his and his colleagues' struggles with finding girlfriends. At the blackboard they began theorizing about why they were having difficulty finding girlfriends, and eventually they landed on the Drake equation, which is a method for estimating the number of planets in the universe that could have life on them. It's a theory that uses the process of elimination to narrow down options to a smaller set of viable options, and so you might start with something easily identifiable, like a star (e.g., the earth's sun).

If there are no planets around those stars, then you eliminate those stars; or if those planets are too close to or too far away from the sun to sustain life, they are eliminated. By applying these criteria, one is able to quickly narrow down the range of possible planets that could sustain life.

Now a correspondent for National Public Radio, Kestenbaum described his and his colleagues' application of the Drake equation to the issue of finding a suitable girlfriend on the radio show *This American Life*. He and his colleagues began by identifying the population of possibilities, which was the six hundred thousand people living in Boston. They quickly realized that if you were a heterosexual man, then you had to cut that number in half, because roughly three hundred thousand of those six hundred thousand people living in Boston were men. If they applied a criterion of women who were between the ages of twenty and forty, then the field of three hundred thousand narrowed to about one hundred thousand. Adding the wish for women with a college degree eliminated seventy-five thousand of the one hundred thousand eligible women. What they realized, just as Anna and I did in our high school library, was that making three wishes for certain traits in romantic partners had quickly narrowed their field of candidates. In this case, from six hundred thousand to twenty-five thousand, which is a reduction of 96 percent from the original field of candidates.

Consider the following example to see how quickly it becomes improbable to find a person with the traits you want. Choosing someone average (fiftieth percentile) on three different traits would narrow a field of one hundred potential mates down to thirteen potential mates. Wanting a partner in the top fifth percentile on three traits gives you just a one in ten thousand chance of finding that partner, and if you do not find that partner, then what do you get? Not only do most people not get whatever traits they prize the most in romantic partners, but they are also then left with a partner possessing a haphazard collection of traits. Maybe you get lucky and get a partner who happens to have a pleasant constellation of traits, but then again, maybe you are not so lucky.

How Different Levels of Traits Affect the Odds of Finding a Partner

Percentiles	Odds	Example Height	Income	Attractiveness
50th x 50th x 50th	13 in 100	5'9"	$35,000	Average
30th x 30th x 30th	3 in 100	5'11"	$60,000	Attractive
20th x 20th x 20th	1 in 100	6'0"	$87,000	Attractive
10th x 10th x 10th	1 in 1000	6'1"	$100,000	Very Attractive
5th x 5th x 5th	1 in 10,000	6'2"	$150,000	Very Attractive

If a fairy godmother suddenly appeared and granted you three wishes for an ideal partner, then how would you spend your three wishes? Wisely wishing for the traits could greatly increase the odds of having a satisfying and stable relationship. The best strategy is to know the odds, accept the limitations placed on partner selection by those odds, and then make the best decisions possible to get the three traits you want the most in a partner.

Consider the following analogy to see what happens when selections are made under a set of constraints. When I was a child, I dreamed of winning a sixty-second shopping spree sponsored by Toys"R"Us. My parents patiently listened as I engaged in a stream of consciousness speech regarding the dozens of toys I would get when I won. They were kind enough not to ruin my wild imagination by telling me that I could never get all those toys in sixty seconds. Had I won the shopping spree, the predictable result would have been me grabbing the first toys I saw, only to run out of time before getting the toys I wanted the most. Similarly, singles often have fairy-tale dreams of soul mates, while ignoring the constraint of three wishes for traits. This translates in practice into grabbing partners based on the traits they first see, which leads to them not getting the traits they most need.

From a psychologist's perspective, the best thing about a fairy godmother granting three wishes is that it makes the recipient of those wishes pause and think carefully about what really matters when selecting a partner. Even if the fairy godmother was suddenly called away to another case before granting your wishes for an ideal partner, the process of taking the time to think through which traits are important and why would probably improve your partner selection and increase the chances that those wishes would come true. As we will see in the next chapter, we need to be very careful about how we spend our three wishes.

Wishing Wisely

On the fifth day after Christmas Eve, Anna discovered for the first time in her life that getting your period can be sweet, sweet relief. During those five days of uncertainty, Anna learned from her intensive research on the topic of pregnancy and childbirth that contraception is worth the hype it receives, that fertility rates fluctuate throughout a month and that raising a child requires quite a bit of money.

She also learned that Jake could not be relied upon during times of stress. When Anna explained to Jake why she might be pregnant, he stopped answering her calls and avoided her at school. Although nothing would excuse Jake's behavior, the trait that best accounted for his flighty behavior was not malevolence, but rather his tendency to become overwhelmed under duress—a trait opposing defensive coordinators would eventually figure out from analyzing game tape. Knowing that Jake's ability to take decisive action became paralyzed when he was under pressure, opposing defenses began to dial up aggressive blitzes, which overwhelmed his ability to understand complicated zone defenses. Given how overwhelming being in Anna's world could be, and given Jake's tendency to become disoriented under pressure, a long-term relationship would have been disastrous.

Anna's story ends simply. I suppose that is the point. She broke up with Jake, waited before rushing into another relationship, used that time to figure out what went wrong and prioritized those traits she really needed in a partner. Then she found a partner with her revised set of traits, a partner who fit seamlessly together with Anna's odd and wonderful set of traits. It was so elegantly simple, so efficient, so Anna. As often happens after stressful life experiences, Anna grew in small but important ways.

The last time I saw Anna was a fall day when I visited during her second year of law school. On a crisp New England morning, we sat in the bleachers, cradling hot lattes, eating scones and watching her new boyfriend play intramural soccer. He looked unathletic, and his functioning on the field followed his physical form. Anna described him as "cute," which in the continuum of physical attractiveness falls far short of "hot." He was Lutheran. Yet he possessed other traits that consistently made Anna so much happier, so much more at peace. For Anna, he was like a dozen doughnuts.

Wishing for the Wrong Partner

CHAPTER 3

Why We Squander Our Wishes

My academic introduction to romance happened during my junior year of college. Bored with the rote memorization and multiple-choice tests in my regular coursework, I decided to enroll in an independent study of the piano, hoping for some kind of intellectual spark. Every Friday afternoon I walked down into the catacombs of the School of Music and into an alternate reality with Lydia, the doctoral student assigned to make me somewhat serviceable at the piano. I always found her sitting in the tiny practice room. The soft white light from the lamp above the sheet music and the cascade of chiffon, lace and silk clothing draped around her gave her an ethereal aura. She would have been at home in an eighteenth-century European concert hall, but against the grunge nihilism of the early 1990s, her style was uncomfortably ironic.

My year studying with Lydia provided me with a rich education in music, history and the origins of our modern romantic conundrums. She was a masterful teacher and possessed an encyclopedic knowledge of 1800s European music and history, particularly the romantic era, which began around the end of the 1800s. She was fully intent on creating a well-informed student, even if the student was a novice like me, and so every piece performed was accompanied by stories about the historical context surrounding the composers and how those contexts influenced their music. Many romantic era composers drew strong inspiration from their love lives, including maddening states of infatuation, tumultuous romances and the heartache of love lost.

My favorite story was relayed to me after my lifeless rendition of a Chopin march. Lydia was clearly impatient with how my lack of passion had insulted this beautiful work of art, and abruptly shooed me away from the middle of the bench. She pushed up her hipster glasses and sighed deeply before playing the piece with the amount of emotion and urgency it deserved. She began recounting the turbulent love life of Frédéric Chopin, a man who fell into a passionate and exhilarating relationship at the same time that the romantic era would begin changing love and marriage in dramatic ways.

Frédéric Chopin stood five feet tall with his bouffant hairdo and weighed about a hundred pounds. The ruffles of pirate-like shirts burst through the lapels of his well-tailored suits and pristine white gloves protruded from his coat sleeves. His compositions arrest the attention of even the most casual listener with their thundering chords that march toward seemingly ominous ends, while a delicate melody floats above, imbuing them with an irresistible beauty. The composer Robert Schumann captured Chopin's compositional blend of power and delicacy, calling it "a canon buried in flowers." Chopin's ability to evoke passionate emotion with bewitching artistry made many hearts ache with desire.

In 1836, Chopin attended a Parisian gala where he met Amantine Lucile Aurore Dupin, one of the most influential authors of the nineteenth century. She is better known by her pen name, George Sand, a name in line with the bold challenge she issued to nineteenth-century gender norms, with her shocking behaviors, such as smoking and wearing men's clothing. In portraits, her individual facial features appear pleasingly proportional but taken as a whole, they evoke a sense of discordance. Although her appearance was considered rough around the edges, few could deny the opulence of her prose. French literary critic René Doumic described Sand's writing as being like "... those rivers which flow along full and limpid, between flowery banks and oases of verdure, rivers by the side of which the traveler loves to linger and to lose himself in dreams."

When Chopin and Sand stood pirate shirt to pirate shirt for the first time, it must have been a peculiar and sensational sight to behold. The sheer stardom, creative potential and baffling chemistry between Chopin and Sand must have been apparent to their fellow guests. They initially pushed away their mutual attraction through outward displays of disgust, with the dismissive air that children assume in the presence of their playground crushes. Love waits for no one, so after a few months of halfhearted resistance, Chopin and Sand fell madly in love.

One can only imagine a typical evening at Sand's mansion in the French countryside. Chopin at the piano, sending arching melodies soaring through the ornate ceiling to the second floor, where Sand sat at her desk, penning idyllic love stories by candlelight. The passionate love generated between Chopin and Sand embodied the ideals of the romantic era, because it was, for a moment, beautiful.

THE DAWN OF ROMANTIC MARRIAGE

Chopin and Sand's love story easily captures our imagination with its seemingly timeless romantic themes, such as the anxiety of a newfound crush, the exhilaration of infatuation and hopes of enduring love. Although anthropological studies suggest that feelings of passionate love have always been part of the human condition, the romantic era was the fulcrum point when beliefs about marriage tipped toward a radical idea. For the first time in the five-thousand-year history of marriage, people began to widely believe that passionate love was not just a happy accident of marriage, but rather *the* reason to choose someone as a marital partner.

The reasons behind this dramatic shift from marrying for survival or economic reasons to marrying for love are somewhat less than intuitive. There were significant changes in life expectancy, reproductive health and wealth around the time of the romantic era that were beginning to make it possible to marry for something as luxurious as passionate love. Although this sounds perfectly romantic, the freedom to marry for passionate love has always been more complicated than one might think.

Part of modern singles' difficulties with finding enduring love is that the goal of marrying for love emerged so quickly, and rather recently without Mother Nature sending out so much as a memo or a tweet to alert anyone to the changed rules. This has left modern singles with little guidance about what the rules of the mating game are, which makes it very difficult to play the mating game well. Delving into the story of how marriage changed 150 years ago can help us see how modern love became a tangled web of needs and emotions. Viewing the original goals of human mating against the backdrop of new expectations of marriage for modern singles will greatly aid our ability to understand why we are prone to squandering our wishes for partners' traits.

To give you a sense of how recently and abruptly these changes occurred, consider what it would be like to learn one set of rules for

97 percent of a game, only to have the rules suddenly change during the last 3 percent of the game. For example, what would happen if two football teams played fifty-eight minutes of a sixty-minute game with one set of rules and then the rules changed without their knowledge during the last two minutes? The players would play on, but without a clear sense of the changes to the rules, their efforts would be misguided and the whole game would begin to look clumsy. Consider another example, that of an elementary school class practicing for a standardized test slated to take place at the end of the school year. What if additional standards were added to the test and the time limits were changed dramatically on the 160th day of a 165-day school year? A small percentage of students might manage to pass the test, but the additional demands and the new time limits would confuse even the best of students.

In this chapter, we'll examine the rules of the mating game during the first 4,850 years of marriage and why those rules changed so dramatically just 150 years ago. In the end, we'll see that the amount of time to play the mating game has increased and the level of difficulty has decreased, but that these advantages have been canceled out by confusion about the goals of the mating game, which creates chaos for singles trying to solve the modern mysteries of love.

THE MATING GAME BEFORE THE ROMANTIC ERA

Let's begin with a fundamental rule that has remained constant throughout history and remains in place to this day: no mating, no species. Accepting this rule does not preclude beliefs about mating relationships, beliefs related to spirituality, diverse sexual orientations or hopes of finding happiness. However, the reality is that any species needs to accomplish the following goals to avoid extinction:

1. Live to an age when you can mate.

2. Attract a partner and have offspring.

3. Nurture those offspring to a reproductive age.

One way to think about these goals of mating is to consider that the purpose of the mating game is to have grandchildren. If your children successfully find a mate and have children, then you derive some confidence that your family, and the human race as a whole, will survive. This may sound silly in a modern age when overpopulation is more of a concern than extinction for humans, but until recently, achieving the goal of raising children to an age when they can successfully reproduce has been far from guaranteed. That's because getting one's basic needs met during the thousands of years preceding the mid-nineteenth century was incredibly difficult.

Abraham Maslow, an influential psychologist in the 1950s, proposed a theory of motivation, known as Maslow's hierarchy of needs, that provides a nice framework for thinking about the forces that shaped human mating over time. According to Maslow's hierarchy, humans strive to meet their needs in succession, beginning with the basic needs required for survival, such as food and water, then moving up the hierarchy to safety needs, social needs, and esteem needs, and then finally to the highest-order need of reaching their full potential, a psychological state of "self-actualization." For thousands of years, humans struggled with just finding shelter, clean water, sustainable food supplies and safety from warring factions or predators. The difficulty of meeting these basic needs, of staying alive, led humans to orient their primary goal of mating around these very basic needs.

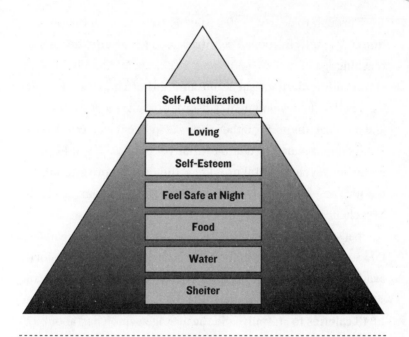

FIGURE 3.1
Maslow's Hierarchy of Needs.

Staying Alive

An eminent group of researchers, led by Sir Roderick Floud of Gresham College in London and Robert Fogel at the University of Chicago, has spent decades developing a program of research that gives us a vivid look into the mating environments during first 4,850 years of marriage. Until the mid-1800s, life expectancies were typically below forty years of age and only one in three children lived to see their fifteenth birthday. These short life expectancies were attributable to a combination of unclean drinking water, sporadic access to food, epidemic disease and widespread violence.

Through the early 1800s, roughly 10 percent of the population in Western European countries died from starvation before reaching age fifteen. An additional 20 percent of households were chronically undernourished, and children born into these families were at risk for developmental disorders, such as low intelligence, and physical illness. So, if there was a 30 percent chance that your family might starve to death or that your children would suffer enduring developmental problems, then your motivation in the mating game was simply to find a mate who gave your family the best chance of surviving.

Let's take satisfying the basic need for food as one example of how tough it was simply to survive. The average number of calories available to the average person in the early 1800s was 2,118, and someone living a very sedentary lifestyle in that time period needed 1,843 calories to stay alive. So the average person had about 275 extra calories to be used for work or leisure activities. However, in doing the work that needed to be done to meet basic needs, the average person quickly burned through this small surplus of calories. In the bar graph, you can see how many calories were required to do thirty minutes of activity necessary for meeting basic needs, including farming (195 calories) or chopping wood for a fire (248 calories). To put this in a modern-day perspective, having only 275 extra calories available for work would mean that going to yoga class for one hour would necessitate being on bed rest for the remainder of the day to avoid starving to death.

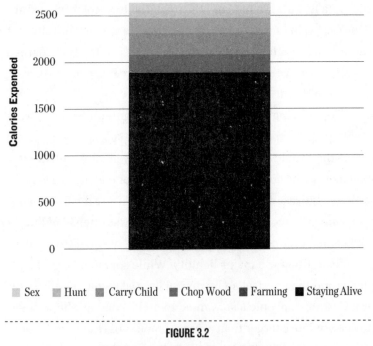

FIGURE 3.2
Calories needed for various activities.

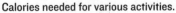

So until the mid-ninteenth century people were faced with managing the following conundrum: they were low on energy, but they needed to expend energy in order to get more energy. This cruel paradox is similar to the problem of seeing your gas gauge hit empty while you're driving in the middle of a long stretch of a barren and unfamiliar highway. A tinge of anxiety rises in you because the next gas station may be two miles away or fifty miles away. You need to get more energy to drive more, but driving to get more energy expends energy. The need to conserve gas while doing the things necessary to get more gas eventually begins to consume all your attention.

When you're low on gas, any mechanical problems with your car, such as a leaking gas line, has the potential to become a big problem. You begin to wish you had a bigger gas tank or a more efficient car. When something like gas becomes scarce, it tends to sharpen your focus on avoiding a drain on your resources and increasing the amount of resources available.

People living in environments with limited resources were highly motivated to find mates who weren't susceptible to health issues that would drain their energy. They were also motivated to find mates who could increase the amount of resources available, which, in the case of something like food, would give them the energy to secure even more resources. A mate who was often ill or hurt or had some other condition that would prevent them from caring for the family was a major liability. While someone with the genetics and the physical ability to use limited resources efficiently was desirable, people also wanted to find someone who was able to accumulate a larger than average amount of resources through hunting, gathering or social power. However, even thousands of years ago, a good man was hard to find.

Finding a Good Mate

Finding and attracting a good mate could increase a family's chances of survival. However, there were few mates available because people lived in small groups, whether in hunter-gatherer groups or small agricultural groups. There were as few as twenty-five to fifty people in a group. Only a handful of those in the group would be available as mates at any given time, which is a bit like attending a small rural school and trying to find a homecoming date. To be extremely generous, imagine that among single young people, there were fifty single mates available in a group. Let's see what happens if an individual made three wishes for a modest set of traits in an ideal mate.

The first wish would be for someone above average in height, or five feet eight inches tall. Height was a reliable marker of physical health in preindustrial societies because nutritional deficits, disease and other health risks were correlated strongly with health and longevity. A second wish for someone who could do an above-average amount of work, nine hours per day, would be a well-spent wish because that work should produce some of the resources needed for the family's survival. Wishing for someone who was five-eight would eliminate 80 percent of the fifty available mates, and only 10 percent of the people would have access to the calories necessary to work a nine hours per day, narrowing down the remaining potential mates from ten to one. Forget about wishing for a brunette versus a blonde or finding someone who wore fashionable fur vests versus leather vests. Just finding someone who could work a full day was hard enough.

	Traits	Percent Meeting Criteria	Number of Mates Available out of 50
1st Wish	5'8" Tall	20%	10
2nd Wish	Work 9 hours/day	10%	1

Here's where things get interesting. Everyone wanted a mate who could improve their family's chance for survival, which set the stage for competing for mates. To envision what the mating game might have looked like, think about modern reality television shows, which thrive by capturing bad romances on the Jersey shoreline or recording conniving bachelors vying for the affection of a pretty bachelorette. Producers of these real-life dramas do something very clever to create the conflict needed for a good dramatic reality show: they put small groups of horny singles into tight spaces.

Then they wait for the inevitable and delicious growth of interpersonal drama that unfolds as sexual tensions give rise to spectacular collisions of romantic self-interests. Early on in these reality shows, we witness the foreshadowing of the competition to come as the alpha male and the alpha female of the households emerge. Everyone begins to aim at attracting the "best" mate available. Jealousy creates fierce competition, BFFs become frenemies and eventually it seems as if the whole group might implode.

When people lived in small groups, with tight spaces created by limited resources and the need to stick close together for survival, there must have been the same sort of drama and infighting when their mating self-interests were pitted against each other in the mating game. However, unlike the drama that takes place on *Jersey Shore* or *Big Brother*, the reality for our ancestors was that the energy expended on relationship drama took away from the energy that could be spent on gathering the resources needed for survival.

In an un-refereed mating game, when unmitigated selfishness, jealousy and hatred run amok, everyone is at risk of losing. Thus someone came up with the clever idea of formulating rules for mating in an attempt to bring some order to the competition for good mates. In an effort likely aimed at decreasing the potential for distractions caused by interpersonal drama, the institution of marriage came into being about five thousand years ago.

In her book *Marriage, a History,* Professor Stephanie Coontz explains how marriage has helped societies live more harmoniously for most of the five thousand years that the institution has existed, which was particularly important when individuals' survival depended upon the seamless cooperation of small groups and when the competition for good mates was particularly intense. The marriage process included having the parents of young people serve as the equivalent of brokers or agents who arranged marital "deals." In these marital deals, daughters' hands in marriage were exchanged for property, livestock or money from the husband's family. One of the primary goals for families was to arrange a situation that increased the amount of resources or the social prominence of the family, which would enhance the likelihood that the grandchildren would be provided for and would possess a lineage that would make them fit to be good mates.

Raising Healthy Children

If someone had their first child at seventeen years of age and wanted be around to help their children find a mate and have children, then the percentage of people in a society living to thirty-five years of age would be a good indicator of mating success. In France during the early eighteenth century, there was a 27 percent chance that your children would die before reaching age seventeen and a 45 percent chance that they would die before reaching age thirty-five.

Remember that the fundamental goal of mating has always been to pass along *your* genes, to nurture your children and then to ensure that your children have children. Given the possibility that children would not survive to a reproductive age, there was great pressure to choose a mate who would improve your children's chances of survival. So you needed to find a mate who was best fit to help you reach this goal. If you frequently saw people around you dying from illness, then it would make sense to choose a partner who looked healthy. Similarly, if you were often hungry, so hungry that you or your children might starve, then it would make sense to choose the partner with the most food. So the best choice of a mate was someone who looked healthy and who had the resources to give you and your offspring the best chances for survival.

Researchers use the term "reproductive fitness" to describe potential mates' physical and psychological health as they relate to their chances of mating successfully and their children's chances of one day mating successfully. When there was a significant chance that your children would not live to a reproductive age, the primary goal was to choose the most reproductively fit mate possible, because that mate would be more capable of providing resources, such as food and protection. Reproductively fit partners would also pass along "good genes" (e.g., strong immune systems, physical strength), which improved children's chances of survival. Through informal observation, it's easy to see that in general, tall parents tend to have tall children, attractive parents tend to have attractive children and emotionally stable parents tend to have emotionally stable children.

Mates are attractive when they possess *physical* traits that are indicative of reproductive fitness, but *psychological* traits are also related to potential mates' reproductive fitness. There are hundreds of studies and many theories to explain preferences for mates with certain personalities, abilities or values. For example, women show a stronger preference than men for potential long-term mates with kind personalities. Although both sexes view kindness as desirable women, who are faced with the "burden" of pregnancy, childbirth and child rearing, would be more inclined to select kind mates who are more likely to form an emotional interest in their well-being and the well-being of their children. Many more findings abound, including preferences for dominant mates, who are more likely to compete well for powerful positions in the social hierarchy, intelligent mates, who are more likely to solve survival problems effectively, and conscientious mates, who are more likely to exhibit a tireless work ethic.

Choosing a mate primarily based on reproductive fitness does not sound very romantic, but one can easily imagine how preferences for reproductively fit traits would evolve in dangerous mating environments. The idea of marrying someone primarily because of passionate love or romantic inklings seems unreasonable when death is so imminent. This is not to say that our ancestors did not feel romantic love, but rather that passionate love was not the primary reason to marry. Then, around the early 1800s, a confluence of events would dramatically change the rules of the mating game.

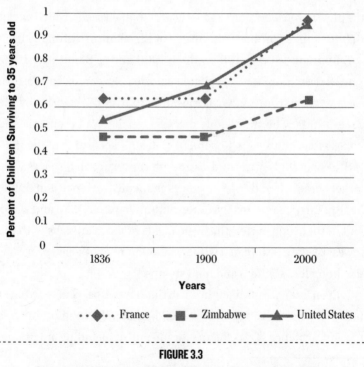

FIGURE 3.3
Percent of children surviving to 35 years old in the early 1800s.

A PERFECT STORM

At the beginning of the nineteenth century, life expectancy in Western European countries was about forty-two years of age, but in the ensuing two hundred years it rose to seventy-seven years of age. In addition, the percentage of children living to thirty-five years of age increased from 45 percent of the population to over 98 percent of the population. The doubling of life expectancy in just five generations is unprecedented in the course of human history and would be remarkable for any species.

These improvements in longevity are attributable to advances in food production, medical care and economic wealth. Agricultural productivity improved dramatically with innovations ranging from the plow to refrigeration to genetically modified seeds, which meant that the time to produce one bushel of wheat or corn dropped from 373 hours in 1800 to 108 hours in 1900 and to 8 hours by 1980. The average number of available calories per person in Western Europe grew from 2,229 calories in 1836 to 2,977 calories by the early 1900s. Communicable diseases, such as tuberculosis and measles, accounted for 47 percent of deaths, according to the 1850 U.S. Census, but by the mid-twentieth century such diseases were largely eradicated due to advances in medical science and public health. Income rose in developed nations between 1836 and 2000, and in that time period the basic needs of more citizens with the fewest resources were met with the development of social programs like homeless shelters and food stamps.[2]

Even infertility is likely at an all time low—8 percent for women under the age of thirty-five—which is probably attributable to a lower prevalence of risk factors for infertility, including nutritional

---

[2] Although those classified as "poor" have better access to some resources through food stamps, shelters and subsidized housing, there is obviously still a great deal of suffering among the homeless and the undernourished. The politics are beyond the scope of this book, but the statement that the position of the poor has improved does not mean the struggles of the poor are fixed.

deficits and disease. Furthermore, medical inter...
assisted reproductive technology, now make infer...
for 42 percent of women under the age of thirty-five.

In the early nineteenth century, wishing for a partner w...
five feet eight inches tall and who could work nine hours a da...
duced the number of mates available from fifty to one. In 2010, those
same two wishes in the United States would reduce a pool of fifty
potential mates to sixteen options. In addition, consider that over
80 percent of people now live in urban areas, compared to less than
10 percent in the early 1800s, which means that there are far more
than fifty initial options available. So not only did life expectancy
to a reproductive age begin to soar, but the number of viable mates
in close proximity dramatically increased.

	Traits	Percent Meeting Criteria	Number of Mates Available out of 50
1st Wish	5'8" Tall	67%	33
2nd Wish	Work 9 hours/day	50%	16
3rd Wish	More than $2,500 in wages	94%	15

The dramatic changes in the rules of the mating game happened
quickly and were caused by events that were far removed from the
daily life of the average person. It would be unusual for individuals to think about how changes in agricultural yield or preventable
disease are potentially influencing their romantic relationships.
So it's no wonder that it's less than intuitive to think about how
historical contexts influence our lives and the partners we choose.
The dramatic changes surrounding mating and partner selection
have changed the rules of the game, and for you to play the game
better, here's a summary of the major changes to the rules.

1. The length of the mating game increased by 83 percent (from forty-two to seventy-seven years).

2. The odds that your children will reach a reproductive age more than doubled (45 percent to 98 percent).

3. Singles began to freely choose their marital partners.

4. The cultural goal for marriage increasingly shifted toward marrying for love.

In the end, this swirl of societal and technological progress produced unprecedented increases in reproductive fitness, which brings us to an interesting question. If the primary goal for thousands of years was to choose a reproductively fit mate, because survival was uncertain, what happened when the odds of survival were virtually guaranteed?

MORE IS NOT ALWAYS BETTER

Investing tends to yield rewards or returns. Watering plants helps them grow, and investing time in your work yields a paycheck. However, sometimes investment hits a plateau, which leads to marginal or even diminishing returns. Plants need water but can begin to die when watered too much, and studies on the workplace show that productivity begins to decline past five hours of effort per day, and in some cases putting in too many hours at work can lead to mistakes (e.g., for air traffic controllers). The point where investing in something is no longer profitable is what economists call the "point of diminishing return." In the same way, investing in traits that predict reproductive fitness may begin to produce diminishing profits for your happiness. One of the best illustrations of the point of diminishing return is that offered by alcohol consumption.

After a drink or two, most people begin to feel a slight buzz, which is a combination of diminishing anxiety, social lubrication and a hint of euphoria. They may continue to feel good after their third or fourth drink, depending on their tolerance, but with additional drinks, things start to go sharply downhill. That's when people go from fun to sloppy, and their moods from euphoric to sad, disoriented or belligerent. This downward spiral continues even after the drinking has stopped. People go for spins in their bed, text their ex-partners something shameful and resort to having their friends hold their hair back. Not until the next morning do they realize that their investment in drinking alcohol peaked around three or four drinks, and that each additional drink took things further in the wrong direction.

So more is not always better. There also comes a point of diminishing return when selecting mates for reproductive fitness. How healthy or resource rich does a mate need to be before people hit a point of diminishing return in the mating game? In the following line graph, you can see that the point of diminishing return occurs at a very low threshold. In the United States, living to a reproductive age is almost guaranteed, with 99 percent of children surviving to age fifteen. Fulfilling the second task of finding a mate is highly likely, with over 90 percent of U.S. citizens marrying in their lifetime.

So, your return on investment is limited when it comes to investing in traits associated with reproductive fitness, such as partners who look healthy or who have the most resources. Your return on an investment is limited when it comes to reproductive fitness partly because there is a ceiling effect. There's simply less room to improve when mating is successful 99 percent of the time compared to when it's successful only 66 percent of the time.

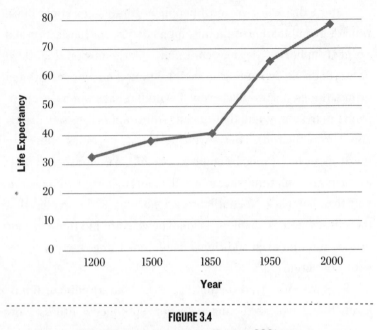

FIGURE 3.4

Rising life expectancy across the past 800 years.

THE RISE OF THE ROMANTIC RELATIONSHIP

As wealthy Europeans saw the threat of imminent death diminish in the mid-1800s, they began to turn their attention to activities done purely for pleasure. When the threat of dying from not having basic needs met began to fade, it no longer seemed superfluous to devote your time and energy to playing piano, writing fiction or lugging a thirty-five-pound gown around at a party. Romantic era intellectuals also began to advocate for people looking for something more than just a cold economic arrangement in their marriages. As the freedom to choose your own partner as a young, single person increased, singles began to seek romantic relationships with the aim of finding personal happiness and passion, and creating something beautiful.

Emotions such as passionate love and happiness have existed throughout human history, but the dramatic advances in life expectancy and greater access to resources freed people to see positive emotional states as the primary goal for marriage, instead of just happy accidents that could occur when your predators were asleep or food was abundant. In the romantic era, the preference to marry for love among the economic and cultural elite of Europe was not only desirable, but a moral imperative. Societies increasingly saw marrying without love as a waste of human potential, a case of citizens not doing their duty to create a passionate and vibrant society. If there is a relatively distinct point in time when the goal of human coupling shifted from living "ever after" to living "happily ever after," the romantic era was that moment.

Although the moment when humans conquered epidemic diseases, began to eat until they were full, and were able to marry for eternal, passionate love sounds like it should have been a triumphant one in the story of human history, this has simply not been the case. Given our current divorce and separation rates, which together hover around 60 percent, and given the 14 percent of couples who are chronically unhappy, it's difficult to argue that the romantics' ideals of marriage have become a reality. How can it be that humans figured out how to dramatically extend life expectancy but did not figure out how to make passionate love endure?

WHAT PEOPLE SAY THEY WANT AND WHAT THEY ACTUALLY DO

The problem with modern love is essentially that couples want to have their cake and eat it, too. Researchers have conducted hundreds of studies investigating what people want in an ideal romantic partner and how these ideals influence the traits they wish for. Some of the laboratory methods used to study partner selection resemble a game, a sort of choose your own adventure in mate selection. Norman Li and his colleagues at the University of Texas at Austin developed a particularly interesting mate selection measure, which can easily be played by following the instructions below.

The table below shows five traits that might be attractive in a potential mate. The numbers on the right are "mate dollars," which correspond to the percentile where your ideal mate would fall in the general population, such that circling an eighty for creativity would mean that your mate would be in the eightieth percentile on creativity, or more creative than eighty out of one hundred people. Imagine that you have only three hundred mate dollars to spend across all five traits, so spending eighty mate dollars on creativity would leave you with 220 mate dollars to spend on the four remaining traits. Circle the number your desire for each of the five traits, while being careful not to go over three hundred mate dollars.

Traits	Mate Dollars										
Creativity	0	10	20	30	40	50	60	70	80	90	100
Physical Attractiveness	0	10	20	30	40	50	60	70	80	90	100
Kindness	0	10	20	30	40	50	60	70	80	90	100
Wealth	0	10	20	30	40	50	60	70	80	90	100
Liveliness	0	10	20	30	40	50	60	70	80	90	100

Now do the mate dollar game one more time, but for this round you are limited to one hundred mate dollars to spend across all five traits, instead of three hundred mate dollars.

If you're like most people, then the way you went about constructing an ideal partner under the three-hundred-dollar condition felt much different than constructing a partner under the one-hundred-dollar condition. Under the three-hundred-dollar condition, if you spent the same amount on all five traits, you would have a partner in the sixtieth percentile for each trait. Being guaranteed a partner who is above average on each trait would add up to a good partner, which obviously makes the game much easier. Guaranteeing someone a partner who is above average on five different traits is also unrealistic.

Assuring singles that they can get more than enough of every desirable trait is like taking a hungry person to dinner at an all-you-can-eat buffet. At a buffet, patrons are guaranteed to get everything they want, and so they are not forced to think about what they put on their plates. Even if someone really wants to eat as much chicken-fried steak, Tater Tots and chocolate cake as possible, they might go to the salad bar first, even if they have little intent to ever eat their salad. Why? Because putting healthy food on your plate gives the socially desirable appearance that you are health conscious and perhaps provides you with the false satisfaction that you are. However, we all know that no one goes to the Golden Corral buffet to stuff themselves with lettuce and quinoa.

Similarly, research participants in attractiveness studies were typically asked to rank order a large number of traits on paper-and-pencil measures, instead of being forced to prioritize a small number of wishes for traits. In an all-you-can-eat scenario, men rate physical attractiveness fourth, and women rank it fifth. Socioeconomic status (resources) ranks near the bottom of both men's and women's list of top ten desired traits. Agreeableness and intelligence, the salad and quinoa of the partner selection world, are among the first three wishes for an ideal mate.

However, real-world mate selection is not all you can eat, and there are hard choices to make. We've seen that you get three wishes for traits in a partner, and then there are the limits of your own "market value." If you aren't a perfectly attractive mate in every way imaginable, then the reality is that some of the potential partners with the traits you desire may not desire you in return. All of this essentially means that you can't get everything you want, and so you might be able to choose a salad or a chocolate cake, but not both. So what do people do when they are forced to choose among a small number of possible traits with a limited budget?

They stuff themselves with physical attractiveness and resources. In one study, Professor Li and his colleagues randomly assigned participants playing the mate dollar game to low (e.g., one hundred dollars) or high (three hundred dollars) "mate dollar" conditions. They found that when female participants were given something close to an all-you-can-eat budget—three hundred mate dollars—they spent a higher proportion of their mate dollars on traits such as liveliness and creativity. However, when female participants were given only one hundred dollars, a more realistic situation that forced them to prioritize what they really wanted, they spent the most on a mate's wealth.

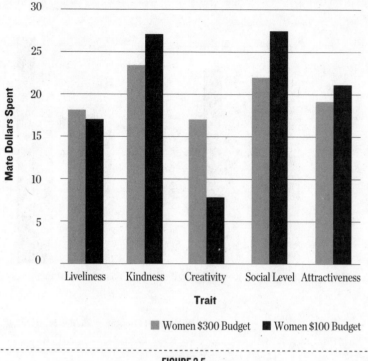

FIGURE 3.5

Percent of mate dollars spent on each trait by women
with a $300 versus a $100 budget.

When male participants' budget was constrained to one hundred dollars, they spent most of their budget on physical attractiveness, as seen in Figure 3.6. Under the constrained condition, male participants spent the second most on kindness and the third most on social level. So, you could say that the top three wishes under the constrained condition for both men and women were spent on social level, kindness and attractiveness.

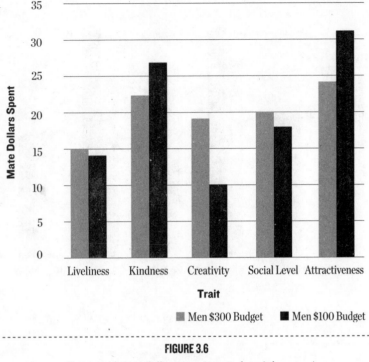

FIGURE 3.6

Percent of mate dollars spent on each trait by men
with a $300 versus a $100 budget.

David Buss is a prominent evolutionary psychologist from the University of Texas who developed Sexual Strategies Theory, which suggests that the tendency for women to spend more on resources and for men to spend more on looks is consistent with the different tasks facing women and men when it comes to reproductive success. The idea is that men are able to produce seemingly endless amounts of sperm on a daily basis, and so theoretically, they could go around having sex with as many women as possible, while not having to worry about long-term commitment. According to Buss's theory, men care most about a woman with "good genes," who would give their offspring the best chance of also being reproductively fit.

Women face a different set of mating challenges because they ovulate once a month, carry the baby for nine months during pregnancy and engage in the potentially deadly task of childbirth, which gives women far more potential "cost" when it comes to having indiscriminant intercourse. According to Sexual Strategies Theory, women should invest more in traits that have to do with a mate's ability to commit to staying around to help raise offspring and to provide resources, such as food and protection.

There are now hundreds of studies that support the idea that during partner selection, men prioritize looks more than women, whereas women prioritize resources more than men, which, along with the finding that both men and women prioritize attractiveness and resources as two of their top three wishes, suggests that traits key to reproductive fitness play a prominent role in mate selection for modern singles. This robust finding is convenient for researchers looking to validate evolutionary theories of mate selection, but it raises a practical concern for outside observers. Why do modern singles spend so heavily on attractiveness and resources when the return on investing in traits associated with reproductive fitness is so low? Would men and women show the same pattern of wasteful wishing for traits when choosing an actual romantic partner?

DATING IS MORE THAN JUST A GAME

We've seen that participants forced into more realistic mate selection situations start to maximize the amount of physical attractiveness and wealth in potential partners and place less emphasis on personality and abilities. There are various approaches researchers take to assess mate selection under more realistic circumstances, which include evaluating behavior at in-person mixers for singles and in online dating and looking at how much partners 'match' on levels of physical attractiveness and wealth.

How we select our partners, when we might actually go on a date with someone, rather than how we choose a hypothetical partner in a laboratory study, was first taken up in a classic study in the 1970s. College students attending a "school dance" completed measures of personality and intelligence and were rated by research assistants for physical attractiveness. At the end of the dance, after the attendees had mingled with a number of their opposite-sex peers, the researchers asked them to rank order the top five people with whom they would like to go on a date. What they found is that the clear determinant of who was *actually* selected as a desired date was neither personality nor intelligence, but rather physical attractiveness. Recent studies of online dating that track what people pay attention to when reviewing profiles have produced a parallel set of findings for cyber singles. It probably comes as no surprise that the most visited links on dating profiles are the photos and the occupational status sections.

Another interesting method for inferring whether singles place a high priority on certain traits during partner selection is to look at how similar couples match up on a variety of traits. Finding no similarity between partners on a certain trait might suggest that singles don't care much about that trait and so they end up with a random level of that trait because of their unintentional approach. Conversely, finding strong matching between partners might suggest that people try to maximize the amount of that trait they get, relative to where they stand on that trait themselves or their own "market value" on that trait. In studies examining the similarity between partners on personality traits, researchers find weak associations for traits such as extroversion, kindness and anxious mind-sets toward relationships.

However, when it comes to physical attractiveness and wealth, couples show moderate to strong similarity. Alan Feingold, a researcher at Yale University, conducted a meta-analysis of physical attractiveness studies looking at the degree of similarity between romantic partners. Feingold found a moderate to large degree of similarity between romantic partners' physical attractiveness, which suggests that individuals might be making a concerted effort to ensure that they get a mate whose level of attractiveness is as close as possible to their own. Other studies have found moderate to large similarities between partners on levels of education, which is a good indicator of overall socioeconomic status.

What these assortative mating studies collectively suggest is that singles' mating selection strategies probably give them a good chance of finding partners who are about as attractive as they are and who have achieved the same socioeconomic status. However, when it comes to personality or abilities, what the singles get in a partner is random. For example, the odds are equally good that they will get partners with a similar personality, a better personality or a worse personality than their own. The results in the chart that follows suggest that extroverts are actually slightly more likely to end up with someone who is a little more introverted and that there is little similarity between partners when it comes to something like levels of kindness. However, when it comes to attractiveness and education level, the degree of similarity is much stronger, with pretty people ending up with pretty partners and highly educated people ending up with highly educated partners.

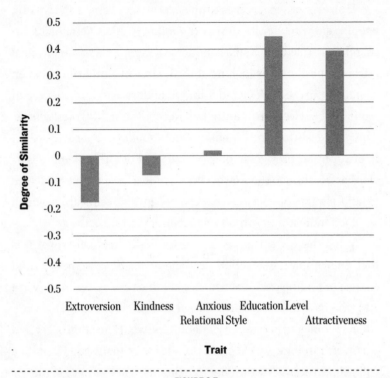

FIGURE 3.7

Degree of similarity between spouses on various traits.

Some researchers have made an astute distinction between what people might want from short-term mating situations (e.g., one-night stands) versus long-term mating strategies (e.g., the father/mother of my children). Physical attractiveness is emphasized more strongly when people are asked about traits they would desire in a short-term partner versus a long-term partner, whereas traits like kindness or conscientiousness are rated as most important for long-term partners. However, there again might be a distinction between what people say they would prefer to do and what they actually end up doing when choosing a long-term mate.

When you think about your friends who are in serious romantic relationships, how many of those relationships were started because someone thought the other person was cute or hot? Regardless of where people meet, whether it's at work, the park or church, they often narrow down the field of potential mates based on physical attractiveness. From this smaller pool of potential mates, they find someone with whom there is a mutual attraction go on a date, and then a few more, and before they know it, they have invested large amounts of time, effort and emotional energy. As the relationship train picks up speed and travels farther from its origin, it becomes harder to jump off it.

So just as there are psychological forces that impel people to continue to root for sports teams that were once promising but are now perennial losers, people also tend to hold on to partners because they've already put so much time and effort into a relationship. This reluctance to let go of partners who are clearly not going to provide any return on the emotional effort invested in them obviously sounds like a poor rationale for continuing a relationship. Yet how many people do you know who have stayed in unhealthy relationships based on a fear of sunken costs?

Findings in behavioral economic and cognitive psychology often show that the best of us can be irrational when it comes to certain things. For instance, we might be overly optimistic about the stock market, overly pessimistic about the side effects of childhood vaccinations and stubborn about using the same failed strategies to solve recurring problems. In matters of love, we might make a host of irrational decisions, but many of our worst decisions hinge on the tendency to focus narrowly on idealized notions of what a relationship is, or once was, while rationalizing away negative information about a partner or a relationship that would be inconsistent with the idealized views. So early preferences for physical attractiveness or wealth can kick-start a relationship that eventually has enough momentum to turn into a long-term relationship.

We'll see in the next two chapters that modern singles still want to maximize traits for fit mates, even though humans are far less threatened by dangerous mating environments. Modern singles still want to invest in traits associated with reproductive fitness, but they also want to invest in traits associated with romantic era hopes for dizzying levels of eternal happiness in marriage.

Adding the goal of romantic bliss to the goal of reproductive fitness has exponentially increased the number of traits needed from a singular partner to have a chance of reaching both goals. We've seen that under realistic conditions, people try to get the healthiest-looking partners with the most resources, and only after satisfying these requirements do they turn their attention to other traits, such as personality or values, which could be valuable for building happy and lasting relationships. Alas, the conundrum of the modern single is this: how do we balance our urges for *reproductively fit* mates with our psychological wishes for *happy* romantic relationships?

It seems as though all this wishing has led to a case of wanting everything and getting nothing. Even though many aspects of the human condition have improved dramatically in the past 150 years, we know that in many ways the outcomes of our romantic relationships have become more tragic, with so few marriages remaining happy and stable. The real-life tragedy of so many unhappy and unstable marriages contains the two plot elements necessary for a great tragedy: beauty and loss. Losing something mediocre can feel frustrating or annoying, but losing something beautiful comes with a desperate form of sadness. Falling into passionate love can be so intense that it seems mystical and fated. So once that beautiful moment is lost, one might wonder whether something so elusive and beautiful will ever be found again. However, we all know on some level that passionate emotions are, unfortunately, ephemeral. This means that when passionate love is the primary pursuit in long-term relationships, people are usually left with a collection of lovely moments and tragic endings.

PRELUDE TO A ROMANTIC TRAGEDY

When Chopin and Sand first fell in love, they surely felt butterflies fluttering in their stomachs and their heads must have been dizzy with joy. Like any infatuated couple, they wanted to absorb everything about each other, and as they grew closer and more devoted to each other, the result was a relationship that was more substantial but also more complicated. Milan Kundera described this paradox beautifully in his novel *The Unbearable Lightness of Being:* "In the world of eternal return, the weight of unbearable responsibility lies heavy on every move we make." As relationships become closer, the weight of increasing investment and responsibility becomes part of us, and of all the places the weight of love could attach, it attaches directly to our hearts. Thus, along with the romantic era notion that someone can "tug at our heartstrings," there is the postmodern reality that the same person can "rip our hearts out."

From the beginning, Chopin and Sand each saw concerning traits in the other. In a letter to his family, Chopin alluded to his vague concerns about Sand when he wrote, "Something about her repels me." Similarly, in a letter to a friend, Sand wrote, "Chopin is the most inconstant of men. There is nothing permanent about him but his cough." It was not just Chopin and Sand who saw concerning traits in each other; friends and peers also identified many negative traits in both of them. One of Chopin's friends, the French writer Marquis de Custine, once commented, "The poor creature [Chopin] does not see that this woman has the love of a vampire."

Yet Chopin and Sand marched ahead in their relationship, brushing these rational concerns under the rug of romantic era idealism. Chopin and Sand were enveloped in passionate feelings and the pursuit of beauty, which prevented them from seeing the ugly future ahead of them. The philosophical problem with a purely romanticized notion of love is how to deal with the concept of stability. One could argue for creating a passionate and beautiful relationship, even if the relationship eventually goes up in flames, because at least there was a beautiful moment when both people felt so passionate and alive. Whether this is true or not, there is a practical aspect to dealing with a once beautiful relationship that has become unsatisfying or unstable that is entirely unpleasant.

How many of your friends who are "good catches" by objective standards sit alone at night, hoping for a soul mate to magically appear? Even when they come across a potential candidate for the role of future soul mate, they refuse to ask the person out and sometimes even refuse to say hello. We might admit to ourselves that at certain moments, we wish someone would ride up on a magical horse and sweep us off our feet.

How many times have you seen friends or family caught in bad romances, deriving masochistic gratification from trying to save, rather than love, some tortured soul? There is perhaps nothing more tragic than to observe the mistreatment meted out by a manipulative romantic partner to someone who is inherently a good person. A loved one who is kind and full of potential becoming stunted or compromised by a romantic relationship is one of the most tragic transformations in psychology, because there is no outcome as sad as a person's loss of a sense of self. Healthy relationships do not cause people to lose themselves. Healthy relationships affirm or even magnify what is inherently best in a person, create an intrinsic motivation to mitigate one's worst proclivities and provide one with the strength to believe in one's finest talents. Yet so many adults, grown men and women who are smart, rational people in every other aspect of their lives, still fall prey to romantic notions of magical love, which have the makings of a tragic end.

As Chopin's tuberculosis worsened in the humidity of Majorca, where the rain and Sand's virulence were unrelenting, he must have wondered whether the fleeting beauty they had shared together was worth the chronic misery he now endured. Chopin was no saint, either. The Polish poet Adam Mickiewicz, one of Chopin's contemporaries, described Chopin as a "moral vampire." Historians have characterized Chopin as neurotic, obsessed with social status and racist, among other undesirable traits, and these eventually took a toll on Sand and their relationship.

Which party should be blamed more for their romantic tragedy is beside the point, because in the end both Chopin and Sand had to exist in a relationship that was neither satisfying nor stable. The moral of this romantic tragedy is that the signs of a relationship's disastrous future are evident before individuals fall madly in love, painted in the vibrant colors of their problematic traits. Although Chopin and Sand's poor decisions are easily discernible to us as outsiders with the benefit of hindsight, this singular romantic tragedy was merely a prelude to a long line of romantic problems to come, and its distinguishing features still influence our love lives today.

After years of emotional abuse and tumult, Chopin and Sand's turbulent relationship finally ended in 1847. One year later at a London ball, the great Chopin played his last concert for a drunken and inattentive crowd. Then in 1849, at the age of thirty-nine, financially destitute and emotionally broken, Frédéric Chopin died. On the evening of his death, his physician, seeing the end was near, leaned over the bed and gently whispered, "Chopin, are you suffering greatly?" to which Chopin faintly replied, "Not anymore."

CHAPTER 4

Escaping the Beauty Trap

Huggins was engulfed by a fruity, yet aggressive fragrance as he walked through the grocery store doors. His nose followed the scent past the carts, past the floral section and through the produce section, until his eyes rested upon the source of the scent. His eyes grew wide with possibility at the sight of a young woman whose appearance was both disorienting and strangely attractive. Huggins's eyes gazed at her steeply slanted espadrilles and slowly moved up her long tan legs, which met her tiny beige shorts at the last possible moment, making her appear, for a moment, pantless. Beneath her cerulean blue tank top, the miracles of Wonderbra technology had pressed her breasts together with such vigor that the two spheres overlapped like in a Venn diagram. A silver necklace held two silver medallions, which rested peacefully atop all this sexual pressure. The visual and olfactory overload from the hot mess who came to be known as the Produce Princess made my friend, whom we all call Huggins, a dangerous combination of two volatile states: desperation and arousal.

Huggins encountered the Produce Princess during the hot summer of 1998, but I have known him as one of my best friends for the past fifteen years. The best guesses regarding the etymology of his nickname can be traced to our college days, when beautiful women who were drawn to Huggins's affable nature would invite him into their beds. Once he found himself in bed, out of sheer respect and politeness, Huggins would give his hostess a big hug good night and nothing else. If there were a male version of *Sex and the City,* Huggins would be Charlotte. He's a guy who is generally upstanding and venerable, whose romantic missteps seem a little more amusing set against a backdrop of an otherwise competent lifestyle.

Huggins has a stocky, athletic build, and he moves with tremendous quickness at all times, which creates the unintended effect of making him look surprised when he arrives at his planned destinations. So he must have looked particularly alarmed standing in the grocery store doorway with his mouth agape and his flattop pushed backward from the cool air-conditioning rushing out into the August night. Huggins's spell was broken shortly thereafter, when a group of air force cadets politely asked if they might slide by him to get into the store.

Colorado Springs is home to the Air Force Academy, an army base and an air force base, all of which create a significant imbalance of single men to single women. These poor odds for heterosexual men tend to arouse primal mating strategies in them as they look for mates under what biologists call increased "selection pressures." *Selection pressure* is a term used to describe challenges to a species successfully reproducing, which could include threats to offspring's longevity or the inability to find a mate. This dating environment, with its intense selection pressures, leads perfectly reasonable young men to depend on the primal regions of their brains and dating strategies that reek of desperation and too much Acqua di Giò cologne.

Being both desperate and aroused while looking for a date is similar to being both hungry and flush with cash while shopping for groceries. People usually end up regretting their intense enthusiasm. Unable to think clearly owing to the cloying nature of his lust, Huggins opted to follow the Produce Princess around the store until he came up with the idea to engage with her in a way that was less creepy than following her. Like a character in a bad detective movie, he tiptoed behind her, as if this would make his lurking more covert.

Eventually, the Produce Princess began walking toward the checkout line and Huggins began to panic. He had been so transfixed by her beauty that he still had no strategy for approaching her. So with no plan, he stepped into line behind her, waited and tried to think. The beep of each product scanned echoing like a ticking time bomb reminded him that time was running out.

Suddenly, he had an idea. It was more of an intuition or a hunch than a thought, but it was an idea, nonetheless. Huggins realized that he could display his spontaneity, generosity and chivalry in one magical, bold act. He would pay for her groceries. Here was his plan: he would dart to the front of the line and swipe his card before she could swipe hers, and then she would look at him with starry-eyed desire. In the deep recesses of his primitive hindbrain, this strategy made perfect sense. So he prepared himself for action.

When the cashier had finished scanning the items and hit the total button, Huggins, with his athletic frame, launched himself toward the credit card machine, like a wide receiver exploding on the snap of the football. His flattop whisked the chin of the Produce Princess as he sprinted toward the front of the line, where he came to a jump stop, squared up to the credit card machine and swept his card. A smile of exhilaration grew from ear to ear, his heart pounded with anticipation and he looked upward to the angelic face of the Produce Princess. It was at this late moment that Huggins noticed some important details for the first time.

He saw that the rectangular medallions dangling from her necklace were actually the dog tags of her military boyfriend. As Huggins's smile began to go limp, his eyes wandered to the large sparkling diamond on her ring finger and he realized that those tags belonged not to her boyfriend, but to her husband. Perhaps it was no surprise that her wide eyes did not convey starry-eyed desire, but rather a mix of bewilderment and mortification. So there they stood, Huggins, the Produce Princess and the cashier, each of them trying to wrap their head around whether Huggins's bold attempt had been psycho or just stunningly awkward. Appalled by his own behavior, Huggins privately wondered, "What was I thinking?"

BEAUTY AND SURVIVAL

Huggins's grocery store debacle demonstrates a classic problem of the human condition and of efforts to select a partner with the right traits. Nobel Prize laureate Daniel Kahneman and Amos Tversky are cognitive psychologists who have investigated why people make poor decisions. What they have found is that when people are faced with decisions both large and small in consequence, they often act without *consciously* thinking about what they are doing, instead allowing their *intuition* to drive their actions. Only after people act upon their intuitive reflexes, do they look back for a rationale to explain their actions.

The human tendency to take action first and then to look for reasons after the fact permeates almost every aspect of our lives. We are wired to operate that way across most situations because the reflexive "intuition-action" link has a distinct advantage: speed. Being able to make split second decisions about things you encounter that might be dangerous versus safe, or good versus bad, allows you to react quickly to situations that could threaten your survival.

This psychological reflex does not look much different than what happens when a doctor strikes your knee with a hammer and your leg reflexively kicks. You don't consciously think, *I've been hit in the knee with a rubber hammer. It's reflexive, so now I should kick my leg involuntarily.* Imagine another example, in which you find yourself in a friend's new garage down in the swamps of Baton Rouge, Louisiana. When the lights are turned on, you see a brightly colored rope on the garage floor. You immediately jump away while letting out a shriek of terror, before realizing that it's just a piece of rope.

After your friend stops laughing, he or she might ask rhetorically why you jumped away from the rope, and you might say something that sounds entirely well reasoned, such as, "The rope looked cylindri-cal, has a rough exterior and is brightly colored, and so it looked like a poisonous snake." Although all of this sounds perfectly reasonable, none of this reasoning goes on between seeing the rope and jump backing. This deliberate thought does not occur in those moments, because if the rope really is a poisonous snake, then your actions need to err on the side of speed.

Similarly, when Huggins saw the Produce Princess, his intuitive reaction did not leave room for him to think in any kind of *deliberate* way about why he lusted after her. When he tried to access his reason to formulate a plan to introduce himself, he found it difficult to think logically and clearly about how to proceed because his intuition and his emotion overwhelmed his higher intellectual functioning. In the end, there was neither concentrated thought about why he found her physically attractive nor careful deliberation about why he should buy her groceries versus another woman in the store. He was responding with a psychological reflex to a powerful stimulus: physical beauty. Huggins is not alone in this regard. Researchers have found that physical attractiveness can lead to reflexive responses that influence not only our judgments about the sexual desirability of others, but also our judgments about their personality, abilities and values. This leads people to pursue partners based on intuition-based stereotypes about physical attractiveness.

What happens when the decisions we face are not life or death, but we still default to relying upon our intuition when making them, such as when we tackle partner selection? Although the common wisdom to "trust your intuition" is helpful at times, not everyone has great intuition in all situations. Even when individuals think they have great intuition about potential, it never hurts to mix a little intelligent thought with intuition before making important decisions. Given the gravity of partner selection and the impact that the partners we choose will have on the rest of our lives, it's important to consider whether we reflexively jump back from people who appear unattractive or, conversely, jump into situations with people based solely on their physical attractiveness.

It's also worthwhile to withhold judgment about whether selecting a partner based on physical attractiveness is a bad idea. Maybe if singles invest heavily in physical attractiveness, they reap surprising long-term benefits from that investment when it comes to building satisfying and stable relationships? Before we analyze the powerful influence of physical attractiveness during partner selection, let's examine the fascinating lines of research about what we find beautiful and how those prototypes of beauty developed in humans. We'll also see why it is so easy to desire intuitively physically attractive partners in the absence of sound reasoning, and we'll explore the kind of return on investment, that is, the degree of relationship satisfaction and stability that people can expect from spending one wish on physical attractiveness.

WHAT DO WE FIND BEAUTIFUL?

In most partner selection situations, whether in person or online at a dating site, one of the first traits we perceive is the physical appearance of potential mates. Although different people have different preferences for certain "looks" or features in potential mates (e.g., brunettes versus blondes), there are still more commonalities than differences when it comes to preferences for physical beauty. Faces and bodies can be attractive based on any of the following three characteristics: symmetry, the average size and spacing of individual facial features and prominent features, such as men's strong jaws or women's voluptuous lips.

Symmetry refers to how much the right side of one's face looks like the left side. If you look at the faces of stars, such as the singers Katy Perry and Beyoncé Knowles, then you can imagine folding a photos of their faces vertically from forehead to chin and finding that the features on the right and left sides of their faces overlap perfectly. Their ears, eyes, brows and other facial features are roughly the same shape and size and are located in the same place. A leading hypothesis regarding why facial symmetry is considered universally attractive is that asymmetry might signal the presence of dangerous genetic mutations that could lower the reproductive fitness of a mate.

Average means that certain facial features are of average size and are situated in the most central location possible. Take Justin Bieber or Reese Witherspoon. Their noses are not large, not small, but interestingly, they are an average size in the continuum of nose sizes. And those "cute" noses are neither a bit to the left nor a bit to the right, or high or low, but rather sit right in the middle of their faces. Have you ever heard a friends describe their dates' eyes as unusually close together or far apart, or their eyebrows as remarkably thick or unsettlingly thin? Average features are thought to occur in those individuals who are immune to a broader range of diseases. Perhaps the best way to understand why genetic diversity is important is to consider what happens when someone has a homogeneous genetic makeup, which is what happens when brothers and sisters mate and have offspring. Their offspring are at risk of dangerous genetic diseases.

Prominent features are facial features that are exaggerated in size or shape. Researchers call prominent features secondary sex characteristics or hormone markers. Perhaps no Hollywood couple has more secondary sex characteristics under one roof than Brad Pitt and Angelina Jolie. From high testosterone release during puberty, Pitt developed a particularly strong, wide and pronounced jawline. His cheekbones are prominent and his brow ridge protrudes forward, whereas most men possess a brow ridge that slopes backward. If you look at Brad Pitt from the side, his profile is like a flat board with a nose and his forehead is perfectly aligned with the bottom of his chin. Due to particularly high levels of hormones released during puberty, Angelina Jolie developed prominent cheekbones and full lips. The tendency for prominent features to look sexy helps explain why two staples in women's makeup kits are blush, to accentuate the cheekbones, and lipstick, to create the appearance of voluptuous lips.

Symmetrical faces tend to be described as beautiful, faces with average features as cute, and faces with prominent features as sexy. Your particular notion of what is most attractive depends partly on individual preferences. Owing to their personal preferences, friends can have great debates about who is sexy or mysteriously attractive. For example, I have a male friend who has a particular weak spot for women who have large gums. I'm not sure from any kind of scientific perspective where this fetish came from, but even this friend shows preferences for symmetry, averageness and, in this case, a strange form of prominence. Dozens of studies, a substantial number of them cross-cultural, point to the same conclusion, which is that we agree more than we disagree when it comes to who we find physically attractive. Whether participants are asked to judge faces within their own racial category or outside their racial category, they tend to have an automatic preference for faces that are symmetrical, have average-size features and have prominent features.

Many of the same principles governing facial attractiveness apply to determining what kinds of bodies we find attractive. We have a remarkable ability to quickly judge the symmetry of bodies, such as the degree of symmetry of someone's breasts, feet and arms. When researchers measure the size and location of body parts, such as elbows, kneecaps and arms, and calculate their symmetry, their results closely mirror the snap judgments people make about symmetey when giving someone a quick glance and using no formal measurements. Secondary sex characteristic development figures prominently in our judgments of bodily attractiveness. Men who release high levels of testosterone in puberty tend to have prominent features, such as broad shoulders, which combined with a trim waist creates a V-shaped upper body. Women who release high levels of estrogen during puberty tend to have a waist-to-hip ratio that puts curves in "all the right places." Studies have found that regardless of the absolute size of a woman's hips or waist, heterosexual men tend to prefer a 0.7 waist-to-hip ratio. Regarding skin tone, skin that is smooth, hairless and relatively free of blemishes is seen as the most attractive.

The theory behind why we have strong preferences for these physical traits is that physical features provide a way to discern the genetic health of a potential mate for the purposes of having offspring with a better chance of survival. Given the absence of genetic testing, blood work and full medical examinations for most of human history, physical appearance was one way to figure out which potential mates were most reproductively fit in dangerous mating environments. For example, high levels of testosterone or estrogen weaken immune system functioning. If individuals experienced chronically high levels of hormone release during puberty and still managed to survive in a threatening mating environment, then they may have a particularly strong immune system.

That's why it's so hard to buck the strong pull toward choosing mates based on their physical attractiveness. There is some nagging or even alarming feeling inside that when we partner with someone who is less attractive, we are threatening our children's chances of survival. When we take a step back and think about where this primal urge for physical attractiveness comes from, it all seems a little bit silly, and it is. However, it doesn't stop there. Not only do we judge physically attractive people to have favorable attributes when it comes to physical health, but we also imbue them with favorable qualities when it comes to psychological health.

WHAT IS BEAUTIFUL IS GOOD

Most of us probably aspire to look past physical appearance and truly judge potential partners solely on the content of their character, but it's also true that most of us can't help but notice when someone is attractive. So in the interest of having an open mind, let's consider whether even the best of us might be influenced by physical appearance when it comes to judging various aspects of potential mates.

In 1972, Ellen Berscheid and Elaine Walster from the University of Minnesota published a seminal study in the *Journal of Personality and Social Psychology* that illustrated the stereotypes people hold about others who are physically beautiful. The stereotypes about beautiful people were so vast and pronounced that they coined the saying "What is beautiful is good" to describe them. Subsequent research over the decades has shown that these stereotypes have far-reaching implications for who we choose as friends, coworkers and, of course, romantic partners.

Berscheid and Walster recruited thirty male and thirty female undergraduates for their research and told them that they were participating in a study of person perception, a vague description that kept the participants unaware of the purpose of the study. The participants were given three envelopes, each containing a photo of students who, they were told, attended other universities. However, the photos were preselected, such that one envelope contained a photo of someone who was highly attractive, the second of someone who was of mediocre attractiveness and the third of someone relatively unattractive.

What they found was that participants who viewed the attractive photo were more likely than those who viewed the unattractive or mediocre-looking photos to think that the person in the photo possessed a desirable personality, succeeded socially and professionally, and would be part of a happy marriage. The only unfavorable judgment came in the domain of parenting, where attractiveness was associated with lesser parenting skills. Subsequent studies over the past few decades have replicated the Berscheid and Walster study, finding that participants assume that beautiful people have good personalities, intellects and occupational prospects and enjoy good friendships and romantic relationships.

The key is to remember that when researchers examine how people go about selecting partners under realistic conditions, such as by constructing mate games with constrained budgets or live dating situations, they find that looks rank first for men and money ranks first for women when deciding who to go out with on a date.

YOUR RETURN ON INVESTMENT FROM PHYSICAL ATTRACTIVENESS

The main theory about people's preference for physically attractive mates has been that physical attractiveness provides a visual indicator of potential partners' genetic health and therefore of their potential value as mates who will help produce healthy, fit children. We've seen in this chapter that most people also assume, based on the "What is beautiful is good" stereotype, that attractive people will bring other traits to the table, such as sociability and good mental health, which could provide some psychological benefits as a romantic partner. So, there are three "returns" to consider when thinking about whether to invest one of your three wishes in physical attractiveness:

1. Are attractive people more reproductively fit?

2. Is having an attractive partner associated with more relationship satisfaction?

3. Does having an attractive partner decrease the chances of divorce?

Physical Attractiveness and Reproductive Fitness

The theory that physical attractiveness is a visible indicator of reproductive fitness is probably correct to some degree, but there appears to be diminishing returns on physical attractiveness in modern dating environments. That's because the chances of reaching a reproductive age and reproducing successfully are now virtually guaranteed, which leaves little room for improving one's mating success. Jason Weeden and John Sabini from the University of Pennsylvania reviewed hundreds of attractiveness and health studies to see whether facial and bodily physical attractiveness were related to outcomes such as physical health, mortality and fertility.

Weeden and Sabini found that there were few consistent associations between physical attractiveness and reproductive fitness. Men's facial attractiveness was unrelated to their health outcomes. There were also few associations between men's bodily attractiveness and their health outcomes. In fact, one of the hallmarks of male bodily attractiveness, a muscular, V-shaped body was actually related to a higher risk of mortality among men.

For women, links between facial attractiveness and health were not consistently significant across studies. However, for bodily attractiveness, women with a body mass index in the normal range (neither too high nor too low) and a low waist-to-hip ratio did have better reproductive and general health.

The authors concluded that the general lack of a connection between physical attractiveness and health might be attributable to the fact that they reviewed studies conducted with participants living in wealthy nations. Advances in health care, nutrition and life expectancy may have muted the advantages of physical attractiveness conferred to previous generations, when mating environments were far more dangerous. Although there appears to be few strong associations between attractiveness and reproductive fitness in wealthy nations, perhaps attractiveness still confers benefits when it comes to the quality of people's romantic relationships.

Psychological Traits Associated with Physical Attractiveness

Although physical attractiveness does not seem to confer significant benefits for physical reproductive health, maybe there is some truth to the "What is beautiful is good" stereotype. Maybe because of favorable treatment from others, who believe that physically attractive individuals are more intelligent, friendly or competent, physically attractive individuals actually develop a better array of psychological traits. However, it's one thing to judge a hypothetical person who is attractive more favorably on a paper-and-pencil rating scale, but would people go so far as to actually treat others differently based on their physical attractiveness?

To see how people actually act toward physically attractive people versus less attractive people, Mark Snyder, Elizabeth Tanke and Ellen Berscheid constructed a clever study. They invited individual women into the lab and told each woman that she would be speaking with a man on the phone. In another room in the lab, individual men were told by the researchers that they would be having a conversation with a woman on the phone, and they were shown a photo of the woman with whom they would be speaking. However, the photo was not the actual photo of the woman to whom the man would be talking, but rather a preselected photo. Half of the male participants were shown a photo of an attractive woman, and the other half a photo of a less attractive woman.

Research assistants, who were unacquainted with the attractiveness or the personalities of the participants in the phone calls, monitored the phone calls and rated the participants on a range of personality variables. What Snyder and his colleagues found was that when men thought they were talking to an attractive woman on the phone, the research assistants rated those female conversation partners as more sociable, likeable and friendly than when men thought they were talking to a less attractive woman. They also found that the research assistants rated the men who thought they were speaking with an attractive woman as more warm, interesting, humorous and flirtatious. What these results imply is that activating the "What is beautiful is good" stereotype led men to treat their conversation partners more favorably, which in turn made it more likely that those women would act in ways that were more warm, friendly and sociable.

These findings suggest the troubling possibility that because physically attractive people are thought to be good, others treat them better, and this lifetime of favorable treatment leads attractive people to develop better personalities, intellects and social skills. The plausibility of this stereotype influencing traits increases if one considers that infants show a preference for physically attractive faces and grade school children adhere to an entrenched "What is beautiful is good" stereotype, thinking that their physically attractive peers are more likable and nice, and less likely to hit them.

Maybe the "What is beautiful is good" stereotype creates a self-fulfilling prophecy for attractive people, such that they are expected by others to possess desirable traits and so they end up embodying these traits more than less attractive people. Although there are obvious dangers associated with holding stereotypes, sometimes stereotypes can be relatively accurate at reflecting reality, and so researchers have accumulated hundreds of studies to investigate whether the "What is beautiful is good" stereotype possesses some accuracy.

The way that researchers investigate the accuracy this stereotype is by administering a relatively objective set of assessments to measure participants' (targets') actual IQ, personality and happiness and by taking photos of the targets for later use. Then they have raters unfamiliar with the targets' scores on those assessments rate the photos of the targets for attractiveness. Finally, researchers look for a correspondence between the scores from the objective assessments and the ratings of attractiveness for each person to see whether those rated as more attractive also tend to score higher on measures of intellectual ability, desirable personality traits and happiness.

Some findings from a meta-analysis by Alan Feingold are displayed in the bar graph below, with each bar representing the average associations between physical attractiveness and a range of traits. Bars hovering around zero indicate no reliable association between attractiveness and traits. As you can see, physical attractiveness is not significantly associated with higher scores on measures of personality, happiness, ability or social skill.

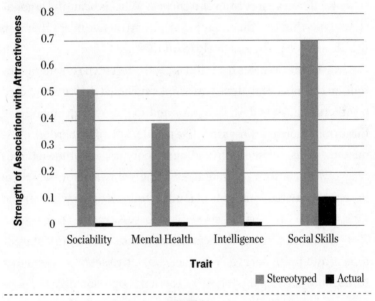

FIGURE 4.1

Differences between stereotyped assumptions of attractive individuals' traits and the actual association between attractiveness and those same traits.

The inclination is to believe intuitively that these findings are common sense. After all, we've been told that we "cannot simply judge a book by its cover." The intuitive response is that *other* people might be shallow enough to spend one of their three wishes on looks, but *I* would never actually make a decision based on how someone looks. Indeed, most of us probably aspire to look past physical appearance and truly judge potential partners solely on the content of their character, but it's also true that most of us can't help but notice when someone is attractive. Although there's nothing wrong with finding aesthetic pleasure in beautiful people, these findings about the inaccuracy of the "What is beautiful is good" stereotype suggest that it would be a mistake to assume that physical attractiveness imbues people with better personal traits. However, physical attractiveness may hold advantages for romantic relationships, and so we turn next to findings regarding satisfaction and stability.

Attractiveness and Relationship Satisfaction

Maybe the aesthetic beauty of physically attractive partners has lasting benefits for relationship satisfaction. You might wake up every morning, look at your partner's natural beauty and think, *It makes me so happy to be in this relationship because my partner is so hot.* Alternatively, maybe the "What is beautiful is good" stereotype confers benefits to the people partnered with beautiful people. Perhaps others assume that just by virtue of being with someone beautiful, you must be particularly sociable, intelligent or successful, which in turn yields more relationship satisfaction, because you are reaping an important return from your partner's beauty.

There have been surprisingly few studies of physical attractiveness and relationship satisfaction, but among the handful of studies I located, the balance of the evidence suggests that there is no reliable association between physical attractiveness and relationship satisfaction. The most rigorous study to date was conducted by James McNulty of the University of Tennessee and his colleagues.

They recruited eighty-two newlyweds and had the partners rate each other's physical attractiveness. They also had research assistants who were unacquainted with the couples rate them in order to have a more objective assessment. What McNulty and his colleagues found was that there was no relationship between either partner's level of physical attractiveness and either partner's relationship satisfaction. In other words, if you are physically attractive, you are no more satisfied in your relationship than someone who is less attractive, and if your partner is physically attractive, you are no more satisfied in your relationship than someone partnered with someone who is less attractive. In fact, the only significant association from McNulty and colleagues' analysis was that more physically attractive men were less satisfied with their marriages.

Attractiveness and Relationship Stability

There are no studies I am aware of that have examined the link between physical attractiveness and long-term relationship stability. In the absence of direct assessments, let's consider whether there are theoretical reasons to believe that physical attractiveness would increase relationship stability. The main benefit of choosing a physically attractive partner is that he or she might be more reproductively fit, which could mean that attractive partners might live longer and provide more stability just by virtue of still being alive. However, in wealthy nations there is no association between attractiveness and longevity. Even if a relationship between attractiveness and health remained, would there be a big difference between choosing a partner who lived to seventy-six years of age versus seventy-eight?

In sum, there is very little long-term return on investing in physical attractiveness for reproductive fitness, relationship satisfaction or relationship stability. Just how little physical attractiveness adds to reproductive fitness or relationship satisfaction is illustrated by the fact that I had to constrain the range of the vertical axis in the following graph to 88 percent to 100 percent. The real range of success on each variable is from 0 percent to 100 percent, but the incremental gain was imperceptible to the eye when graphed using the full range. The primary benefit for people who are more attractive is that their likelihood of marriage increases from 90 percent to 92 percent. Physical attractiveness adds little to one's chances of being reproductively fit, which is partly because of the ceiling effect created by the base rate of surviving to age thirty-five, which hovers around 98 percent. Attractiveness is not associated with relationship satisfaction, and there is no sound evidence or theory at this point to suggest that attractiveness increases relationship stability.

It's worth noting that the limited return on investment in physical attractiveness is somewhat counterintuitive especially in light of some of the research findings reviewed in this chapter. Recall that physically attractive children are stereotyped more favorably than less attractive children. This "What is beautiful is good" stereotype carries into adulthood and actually leads to differential treatment, as physically attractive people receive more favorable treatment than less attractive people. This favorable treatment can generate very concrete outcomes, such as more physically attractive people earning slightly more than their less attractive counterparts.

It's important to remember that despite these advantages, ultimately, physically attractive adults do not end up better off than less attractive adults when it comes to traits and relationship outcomes. Attractiveness does not make people smarter, nicer or more satisfying as romantic partners.

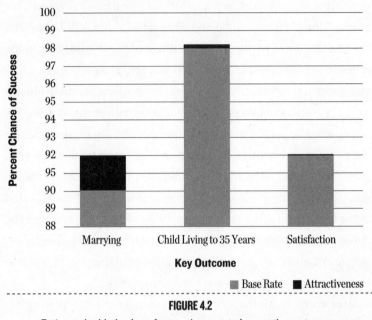

FIGURE 4.2

Estimated added value of attractiveness to key mating outcomes.
Note: Vertical axis constrained to 88–100%.

ESCAPING THE BEAUTY TRAP IS DIFFICULT

Intellectually, the place of physical attractiveness when it comes to partner selection makes perfect sense under the scrutiny of deliberate and reasoned analysis. However, what we have seen from the balance of research findings in this chapter is that people seem intuitively driven to spend one of their three wishes for a mate on physical attractiveness. This lingering tendency to choose a partner based on physical attractiveness is understandable, because for 99 percent of human history, when survival and reproductive success were far from guaranteed, the advantages signaled by physical attractiveness yielded many benefits.

However, the dramatic changes in quality of life for most people in wealthy nations mean that living to a reproductive age and having reproductive success are highly probable. For people living in wealthy nations, there appear to be no discernible benefits from having a physically attractive partner when it comes to reproductive fitness, and attractiveness does not appear to be associated with any benefits in terms of relationship satisfaction and stability. So can we reasonably expect people to completely bypass their intuitive urges to use one of their three wishes for traits in a partner on attractiveness?

This seems unlikely. Although the "What is beautiful is good" stereotype generally leads to overly optimistic assumptions about partners' traits, there is also no overwhelming evidence to suggest that attractive people are more likely to possess undesirable traits, such as vanity or less empathy. In other words, there's nothing wrong with having an attractive partner, but attractive partners also don't help you find happily ever after more than less attractive partners.

So using one of your three wishes to maximize physical attractiveness in potential partners seems like a poor investment, if only because doing so precludes you from getting other traits in a partner that are much better predictors of long-term relationship quality. However, it also seems reasonable to say that kissing your partner should not feel the same way as having to eat your broccoli as a kid. The practical implication is that you want to feel some attraction to your partner, but you need to be thoughtful and to use *reason* when it comes to setting your point of diminishing return.

BEWARE OF INTUITION ALONE

Huggins, despite all his intelligence and his sound character, fell prey to the pressures of the man-rich environment in Colorado Springs. Before he knew it, he was swept away by the smell of sweet scents and lost in a vision of Venn diagram cleavage. For all of us, lust can cloud our ability to see clearly into the future.

I am often asked what motivated me to study the psychology of romantic relationships. Like many people who passionately pursue a given career interest, I study romantic relationships because I have found nothing else so compelling. There are few experiences in life as demoralizing as a broken heart, and conversely, few experiences are as exhilarating as falling in love. Romantic relationships affect our hearts with a uniqueness and intensity that are unmatched by other emotional states. So it is important not to overthink matters of love. However, all heart and little use of one's head is a recipe for disaster.

The way people find enduring love is by applying both heartfelt intuition and clear reason. When we are swept up by the powerful forces of romantic love, experiencing the emotions of infatuation or love is guaranteed, but engaging in judicious problem solving in the throes of infatuation is certainly not. Devising a romantic strategy before being swept up by the forces of love is the best way to ensure that we make intelligent decisions and foster long-term relationships. Probably most of us have, at some point, been swept away in a moment of infatuation, only to be sorely disappointed when we discover we are with someone who is attractive but who possesses a miserable array of psychological traits.

I give Huggins a hard time, but he is a good sport to tell me about his romantic mishaps, such as the Produce Princess. For all he knows, his stories of romantic misadventure could end up in a lecture or a book someday. Although one of his traits is a remarkable proclivity for being awkward in romantic situations, in general Huggins possesses some of the best traits one can imagine. As a friend and family member, he is thoughtful, kind, devoted and fair, traits that will serve him well someday as a husband. I know this due not to his self-promotion or my administration of sophisticated psychological tests, but because across good times and bad times, he behaves with an integrity that is unwavering.

Huggins would never tell anyone, but those who know him well are aware of why he arrives late at night at the grocery store. He often works long hours but does this neither for career prestige nor for money to purchase material possessions, but rather to create a better financial situation for his mother and father, who can no longer work. The same kindness and loyalty are what drive his commitment to mentoring young people in need, and these same traits are what motivated him to drive through a winter storm from northern Michigan to southern Minnesota when he sensed that one of my relationships was going into the tank. It is easy to miss good people like Huggins, because unlike visual traits such as physical attractiveness, desirable psychological traits are not well advertised. They are discerned when we are carefully observant of individuals' subtle and thoughtful behaviors.

CHAPTER 5

Can't Buy Me Love

Some men possess secret abilities: hidden talents not immediately visible upon first meeting them, but that, once manifested, dramatically raise their overall level of attractiveness. Some men have been blessed with the ability to dance, sing, dunk or paint nudes. Conversely, I have been cursed with two left feet, tone deafness, marginal athletic ability and fine motor skills requiring occupational therapy as a child. All of this seemed unfortunate in my early dating years, as I watched other boys waltz and sing their way into girls' hearts, but then a woman I dated in graduate school opened my eyes to my hidden talent. One summer evening I prepared an appetizer with proscuitto and cantaloupe, and after my girlfriend bit into the fragrant, sweet melon, she blissfully whispered in my ear, "You choose the best cantaloupes."

I guess being a purveyor of great melons was not exactly what I had hoped for as a teen, but over the years I have grown to appreciate my hidden proclivity. It says something about my familial roots and the love story that led to my being. Both of my parents grew up on farms, my dad on a cantaloupe farm in the midst of the barren slopes of Rocky Ford, Colorado, and my mother in a small upstate New York town called Genoa. As an aside, my mom's father made a living discerning the biological sex of chickens, an occupation called "chick sexing," which owes to the interesting fact that chickens are not well endowed and require the discerning eye of specialists to assess their sex and thus their value in the marketplace. After my biological grandfather passed away, my grandmother married another chick sexer. Of all the traits...

Anyway, my parents grew up with little money, but both managed to cobble together loans and part-time jobs to put themselves through the University of Northern Colorado. My mother's friend Lynn was dating my dad's friend Mike, and they tried for weeks to set my parents up on a blind date. Lynn finally made her case when she admitted to my mother, "Here's how much I like Bruce. If I wasn't dating Mike, I would definitely be dating Bruce."

One week later, my dad picked up my mom for their first date at a local Italian restaurant. In that candlelit romantic setting, my mother found my dad to be largely unimpressive. He did not have a great sense of fashion, had not been taught to use proper table manners and was about twenty pounds overweight. Fortunately for my dad, my mother has always had one materialistic weak spot: fast cars. Using some of his leftover money from his military service, my dad had purchased a brand-new red Chevrolet Impala, which was Chevrolet's top-of-the-line sports car in 1963. So my mother agreed to a second date mostly because she loved the sound and the feel of that 250-horsepower engine more than my dad's charm.

It's funny that a material possession was the catalyst between my parents' first and second date because my dad had no money at the time and there were no signs that he would ever accrue great wealth. My mother has a natural gift for making accurate predictions about people, and so as she put her hand into the summer night, feeling the cool September air rush through her fingers, she knew that it would be the last time my dad bought a car fast enough to give her the luxurious feeling of speed. Instead, it would be his gentle demeanor, giving spirit and contagious laugh that led my mom to say, "I do" three years later. Those traits also contributed toward sustaining a happy marriage for over three decades.

It was not until the summer after my first year of college that I realized how happily married my parents were compared to many other couples, and how fortunate I had been to grow up in a household with such a satisfying and stable marriage between my parents. As happens in young adulthood, I also realized for the first time that I might want to solicit my parents' advice, instead of stubbornly rejecting counsel from people who might know a thing or two. I asked them when they knew that they had found the person they wanted to marry. That's when my dad told me about the one time they broke up, during their senior year of college, after dating for about two years. They had the biggest fight of their young relationship, and after hearing enough excuses from my dad, my mother told him, "Go home...and take your damn groceries with you."

Even in that moment of anger, my mom cared enough to remind my dad to take the food he kept at her house, knowing that he might not have enough money to eat until his next paycheck came. He wistfully recounted that precarious moment to me:

"So, there's my sorry ass carrying two bags of groceries, trying not to slip on the snowy street. That day the windchill was horrible. My fingers were getting so numb that it became difficult to hold on to the bags, and I felt them slowly slipping from my grasp. That's when I began to feel the tears welling in my eyes. That's when I knew that I could neither love someone so much as I loved your mother nor rely upon someone loving me so much in return."

I remembered this story years later, when I was in graduate school and was buried in a stack of academic journals. I was reviewing data on wealth and marital outcomes, and as I worked through decades of research findings, I saw that the economics of marriage *do* matter when it comes to predicting relationship satisfaction and relationship stability, but as we'll see, wealth matters far less than most people think.

RESOURCES AND SURVIVAL

Have you ever found yourself alone in a secluded location at night? Maybe you got lost while camping and began to panic that if you could not find your way, you would run out of food and water or freeze from exposure to the elements. Or maybe you wandered into a high-crime area late at night, were all alone and feared for your safety. In these situations, when you feel a real threat, your heart races, your respiration speeds up, muscles pulse with tension and your eyes reflexively focus on a singular goal: survival. Although circumstances that threaten our existence can arouse intense survival instincts, even more intense is a mother's response to threats to her children's existence. When offspring are threatened, the hindbrain takes over and a primal drive gives mothers the strength to lift cars off of a trapped child or work three jobs to put food on the table.

Nowadays many people are lucky to live in modern environments where visceral feelings of threat, such as hunger, thirst or lack of shelter are relatively infrequent experiences, which was not the case for most of human history. Nonetheless, the consequences of events that threaten our life are still heavily weighted, which is to say that if we die, all the food, shelter or money in the world doesn't really matter anymore. So just as humans are still relatively hardwired to choose physically attractive partners for their reproductive fitness, they are also drawn to partners with resources, because for most of human history people needed as many resources as possible just to survive.

Recall from Chapter 3 that when participants are put into realistic mate-choice situations, women spend their first wish and men spend their second wish on wealth. What we will see in this chapter is that we have an impressive array of strategies for assessing a partner's earning potential. Singles know that explicitly stating that they want partners who are as wealthy as possible sounds shallow, so they frame their wish for wealth in terms of traits that sound more socially acceptable.

Although some singles may truly want traits like intelligence for the purposes of enlightened conversations by the fireplace or a partner with a college degree so that they might enjoy the benefits of a broad liberal arts education, these also happen to be traits that are associated with higher earning potential. Similarly, wishing for a partner with a personality trait like social dominance might be derived from an admiration of individuals who can take command of a situation and lead, but once again this trait is often associated with higher earnings.

In his book *The Happiness Hypothesis,* social psychologist Jonathan Haidt provides a well-integrated summary of research about why our pursuit of wealth may interfere with our ability to secure personal or relational happiness. Based on a voluminous review of existing happiness research, Haidt suggests that our intuition is to maximize wealth, even when we're far past a point of diminishing return for our personal safety or happiness. We're a bit like squirrels just trying to get some nuts, knowing that one good day of foraging might be followed by three bad days.

Our instinct or intuition is to want more, even when we have enough, and any wise person will tell you this is no way to find happiness. Even if nonessential purchases will create tremendous financial pressure for years to come, people nonetheless find themselves taking on ill-advised debt, thinking that bigger houses, shinier diamonds or faster convertibles can buy them some happiness. This misguided logic gets even more misguided when people decide that attracting a partner who is as wealthy as possible is vital to gaining access to excessive material goods.

There's nothing wrong with wanting someone who is smart, educated, socially dominant or even wealthy. The key is being thoughtful and honest with ourselves about *why* we want those traits, because choosing a wealthy partner does not get us much more than wealth. Just as we assume that potential partners who are beautiful possess other desirable traits, we also assume that wealthy people possess other desirable traits. A survey by researchers at the University of Florida found that young adults assumed that compared to less affluent people, wealthy people have more ability and social sophistication and lead a desirable lifestyle. The only negative stereotype that survey participants expressed was that wealthy people are less considerate than less affluent people. So are wealthy people better or worse romantic partners than those with fewer resources?

THE RETURN ON INVESTMENT FROM WEALTHY PARTNERS

Our intuitive preference for partners with more resources is due theoretically to the fact that for the majority of human history, resources were so scarce that partners who were not great at garnering resources and conferring protection posed a risk to the family's survival. There is still a fundamental need to provide a basic standard of living for your family, but do partners at the high end of the resource continuum yield enough reproductive fitness, relationship satisfaction or relationship stability returns to justify spending one of your three wishes on wealth?

Physical Outcomes and Wealth

In a 2012 Gallup survey of over thirty-one thousand randomly selected people in the United States, 82 percent of participants reported that they had their basic needs met on a consistent basis. One marker of the overall increase in wealth in countries like the United States is the percentage of disposable income available for leisure activity versus income spent on basic needs, such as food. In 1875, the percentage of income devoted to food was 49 percent and the percentage devoted to leisure was 18 percent, compared to 5 percent for food and 68 percent for leisure in 1995.

When the broader history of mating and marriage is considered, it becomes clear that far fewer people struggle to meet their basic needs in wealthy nations. Although a significant percentage of those in wealthy nations continue to battle poverty, hunger and homelessness, safety nets, such as welfare, food stamps and shelters, and technological advances nowadays help prevent the high mortality rates that plagued humans for thousands of years. Resourcefulness, generosity and expanded social programs now provide the assurance that 99 percent of children born in wealthy nations will live to see their thirty-fifth birthday.

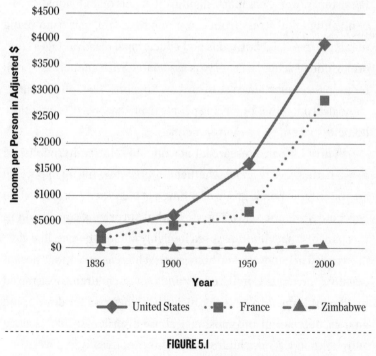

FIGURE 5.1
Changes in income from 1836 to 2000.

According to Maslow's Hierarchy of Needs, when societies can meet individuals' basic needs on a consistent basis, people can turn their attention to fulfilling high-order needs, such as building self-esteem, loving others and self-actualization. It is difficult to argue against the idea that trying to get one's basic needs met on a consistent basis requires a significant amount of attention and causes a considerable amount of distress. However, there are plenty of deeply impoverished people who have better self-esteem and more loving relationships than some wealthy people. So do these unprecedented levels of affluence in wealthy nations correspond to higher levels of psychological well-being and relationship quality?

Psychological Traits Associated with Wealth

Persistent poverty has many significant effects on individuals' well-being, including stress from economic hardship, fear from living in high-crime neighborhoods and educational disadvantages from underfunded schools. Poverty is associated with an increased risk for mood and substance use disorders. So money can influence psychological outcomes by freeing people from the stress of starvation, homelessness or risky environments.

Suniya Luthar, a researcher at Columbia University, published a fascinating review about whether children growing up in poverty are the only economic group of children at increased risk of negative psychological outcomes. The somewhat surprising conclusion in this paper is that children raised in highly affluent homes, like children raised in impoverished homes, are at increased risk for a host of negative outcomes. Compared to middle-class children, those raised in affluent homes are at a significantly higher risk for developing anxiety, depression and substance abuse disorders in adolescence and adulthood. While children raised in economically impoverished environments are at risk because of stresses related to getting basic needs met and safety, children raised in affluent homes are at risk because of the stress from high standards for achievement and from isolation from parents.

The general finding regarding income and psychological health is that there is a U-shaped curve, such that those at the low and high ends of the earning spectrum are at a unique risk for psychological distress. Findings from dozens of studies suggest that when it comes to psychological well-being, there is risk to those living below the poverty line, which in 2012 was set at $23,050 for a family of four. Then a point of diminishing return occurs around a household income of $75,000, such that once this $75,000 threshold is crossed, there is no significant association between more wealth and higher levels of psychological well-being. As we've seen, there comes a point when affluence becomes associated with social pressures and social isolation, which puts children at risk for negative psychological outcomes.

In other words, no added benefit is derived from having a partner who helps you attain a household income of $750,000 versus $75,000. Life is certainly not easy for a family of four who depend on an household income just above the poverty line, and budgets still require some austerity when household incomes are around $75,000 per year, but comparatively, both levels of income are much higher than those of previous generations. Although we've seen that higher levels of wealth do not ensure personal happiness, does having a wealthy partner increase your chances of finding a love story that ends happily ever after?

Relationship Satisfaction and Wealth

When looking to explain in a straightfoward manner the association between economic circumstances and marital functioning, Rand Conger and his colleagues at Iowa State University's Institute for Social and Behavioral Research provide one of the best theories available. Their family stress model of economic hardship contains three basic components: (1) when economic hardship makes it difficult to meet basic needs (e.g., food, shelter), (2) both partners are burdened with increased personal distress, which in turn leads to (3) more negative relationship behaviors when the couple interacts and to each partner feeling more negative about the overall quality of the relationship.

FIGURE 5.2
The family stress model of economic hardship and marital quality.

Conger and his colleagues suggest that there are a number of markers of economic hardship. One marker is falling below the poverty line. It is at this point when government agencies often determine that people are eligible for food stamps or public housing, which essentially means that they might not be able to meet their basic needs. Other markers of economic hardship are male unemployment, large amounts of debt and an onerous work environment.

In the face of these objectively difficult circumstances, partners are more susceptible to anxiety, depression and substance abuse. These personal struggles then affect a couples' ability to function well and they experience increased conflict over financial strains, but each partner also develops a more pessimistic view in general, which may taint his or her views of the facets of the marriage that are unrelated to economic issues. This cascade of personal and relationship dysfunction kicked off by economic hardship can create a global dissatisfaction with the long-term relationship and relationship instability.

A careful reading of the hundreds of studies on resources and marital quality leads to a contingent conclusion: money matters, but only up to a certain point. Researchers who have tested the family stress model have accumulated impressive evidence that economic circumstances are related to marital satisfaction when events place a clear strain upon partners, which in turn affects the functioning of the marriage. In seven large-scale studies spanning different research groups and samples from different countries, researchers found a remarkably consistent link between economic hardship and increased emotional distress in partners, and this distress is then associated with less relationship satisfaction.

The terminology in the family stress model is telling because it implies that a couples' level of wealth does not show a linear relationship with marital satisfaction, such that there is a one-to-one correspondence between every dollar accrued and relationship satisfaction. Rather, as is the case for personal happiness, marital satisfaction depends mostly upon the *absence* of some economic hardship, such as falling below the poverty line, unemployment (especially for men), home foreclosures or large amounts of debt, and once those economic hardships are averted, there is a diminishing return on wealth. The percentage of couples who will experience these types of economic hardship at any particular time is about 20 percent of the general population of the United States. Put differently, there is an 80 percent chance that you will *not* deal with economic hardship that could jeopardize your relationship satisfaction. So if you are playing the odds, then you probably don't need to spend a wish on wealth to ensure relationship satisfaction, but what about wealth and relationship stability?

Relationship Stability and Wealth

The idea of economic hardship being a decisive factor in relationship functioning is very clear when looking at research on wealth and relationship stability. In a longitudinal study of over three thousand women that was published in 2010 in the *Journal of Divorce and Remarriage,* it was found that the odds of divorce during the first ten years of marriage were 2.8 times higher for women in households in the lowest quintile of yearly earnings ($18,400) compared to those living in households in the highest quintile ($264,700). The biggest drop in divorce risk, a 17 percent decrease, occurred once the individual moved up and out of the lowest quintile, which was where the poverty line was situated ($23,500). There was a marginal decrease in divorce risk as income increased past the median levels of income ($64,500), but the gains were small compared to those seen with the jump past the poverty line.

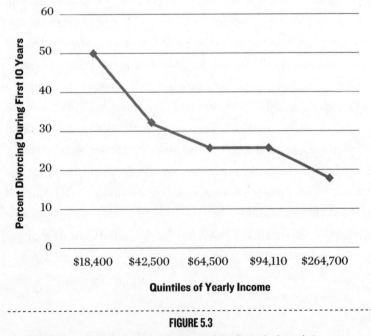

FIGURE 5.3

The chances of divorce based on quintiles of couples' yearly income.

Similar to the relationship satisfaction findings, the key is avoiding economic hardship if possible, as it has a deleterious effect on relationship stability. Once couples cross the poverty line, they reach a point of diminishing return and can expect little return on investment when it comes to marital stability.

So when thinking about wealth and the search for happily ever after, the essential element appears to be finding someone who can help you create a household where basic needs are met and there is a low probability of experiencing economic hardship. The good news is that the odds of finding someone who meets these criteria are high, with roughly 80 percent of potential partners falling above the poverty line. Even though the research findings suggest that wealth is not all it's cracked up to be, would you be fine with living just above the poverty line?

BUT I WANT "THINGS"

The truth for many people is that they want material possessions and they want to live well beyond the poverty line. One need only look at the pattern of consumer spending and debt in the United States to find evidence of our predilection for all things shiny and new. Many people know that the fundamental principle of home economics is that if they spend money on one thing, it means that they might not be able to spend money on something else. The same logic applies to partner selection, because spending a great deal to acquire a partner with a certain degree of wealth may mean foregoing other desirable traits. Sure, it would be nice to live in a big house with shiny things, but there is nothing more demoralizing than feeling alone in a barren, impoverished relationship.

Collectively, the data on economics and marriage suggest that you want to select a partner who will ensure that your household income clears the poverty line with some room to spare. This is a relatively low bar, as 80 percent of your potential partners will clear the poverty line. If you wish for a partner who has yearly earnings of at least $75,000, then you will rule out 70 percent of your potential partners. Its important to remember that the studies reviewed in this chapter are based on household income, which means that if you are working then it's the sum of your two incomes that matters. For example, using the table below we can see that if you work in a Business and Financial occupation, then your partner could work in any of the listed occupations and your household income would clear $75,000.

Occupation	Annual Mean Wage
Food Preparation & Serving	$21,430
Bartenders	$21,550
Janitors	$24,840
Tellers	$25,510
Construction	$38,250
Sales	$37,520
Education, Training, Librarians	$50,870
Business & Financial	$68,740
Computer & Mathematical	$78,730
Physicians	$184,650

There's nothing wrong with wealthy people. It's just that having a lot of money is not a great predictor of relationship outcomes. Once couples pass the point of economic hardship, additional wealth is not a good indicator of whether they will find happily ever after. Rather, it's what people do with what they have that tells us something important about their potential as a partner. What people do with what they possess tells us something about their personality and their character, and these two parts of the equation, as we will see in the coming chapters about how to spend our wishes, hold the key to solving the mystery of finding happily ever after.

THE DIFFERENCE BETWEEN POSSESSING AND GIVING

My dad taught me that the key to choosing the best cantaloupe is looking past what appears polished on the outside. The sweetest melons appear rough on the outside from bugs trying to eat through the exterior, though not all cantaloupes with a rough exterior are good ones. Additionally, when you pick up a cantaloupe for a closer look, if it's a good one, its weight will feel substantial in your hands, and if you bring it close to your nose, the smell will be aromatic. As with cantaloupes, if you choose partners based only on their polished exterior and fail to take a closer look at the traits that are actually important, then you could very well miss out on finding what you really want.

My dad's curiosity led him to figure out certain things during the course of his marriage that were not a part of his impoverished upbringing. Through reading instructional books and being keenly observant of others, he learned how to improve his table manners and he developed impeccable taste in fashion. He was ambitious and highly influential in his work as a teacher. On those first dates together, when my mother was trying to figure out who my dad was and what he would become, she never forecast that he would become a wealthy man, and in the end, she was right. At the time, she reasoned that there were far worse things in marriage than not having a fast car.

One of the hallmark moments of their early marriage occurred right before their first Christmas together. My mother had managed to save some money from their teacher salaries over the previous six months, and on a snowy December day she went to the bank to withdraw some of these savings for a Christmas tree and some gifts. When she handed the teller her check to withdraw the money, she was alarmed to find out that almost all of the two hundred dollars in the account had been withdrawn earlier that day. There was only one other person with access to that account. She drove home with a mounting fury through the falling snow, her impatience with the slow traffic and my dad growing by the second.

She slid to a halt in their driveway, and on her march toward the house, she stopped by my dad's car to retrieve his book bag because she knew he would forget to bring it inside for his lesson planning. With an exasperated swoop of her arm, she cleared the heavy layer of snow from his trunk. When the keyhole was visible, she inserted the key, let the trunk fling open, and then stood in disbelief before a trunk full of socks, sports equipment and coats. In an instant, she knew what my dad had done. Every Sunday my dad volunteered at a juvenile detention center, and the thought of those young men going without an ounce of grace or generosity was too much for him to bear.

Although my dad should have discussed this purchase with her before he spontaneously withdrew their money from the savings account, my mother still found it impossible to recapture any of the anger she had felt over the matter. In fact, as she gazed into the trunk of his clunker car, she found herself falling more hopelessly in love with the man of modest means she had married.

With a pattern of behavior like this throughout their marriage, I was not entirely surprised at my dad's answer to my question about the keys to a great relationship. He began by whispering the following secret across our kitchen table. "I didn't like theater." He had always been more of a sports guy, but for decades, he had not missed an opening night at the theater with my mother. He had spent hundreds of hours watching song and dance at the theater while a "big game" was on the television, and those were the pre-TiVo days. Those nights at the theater were about supporting his wife in something she found joyous and not about vying for "his way." There is no such thing as winning in marriage, because if on some occasion, one partner wins and the other loses, both partners end up losing in the long run.

My dad neither complained nor feigned enthusiasm for those nights at the theater. He knew that if my mother was happy, then he was happy, and that their collective happiness was always more gratifying than the sum of their individual levels of happiness. We don't want to feel that our differences are merely tolerated by our partners, that our relationships are predicated on cold economic exchanges of "one for me and one for you." One of the things that distinguishes great marriages from good marriages is the degree to which appreciation trumps tolerance.

Maybe the risk of choosing a partner based on wealth in the long run is that it places money and materialism in play as primary values in the relationship. When a partner is chosen based on wealth, the thinking going forward in the relationship might be, *I selected you for your money, now you better provide what I expect.* However, the economics of successful marriages are not predicated on a zero-sum game, but instead are built on an unconditional emotional, financial, and lifestyle investment in each other.

PART
THREE

Finding
Happily Ever
After

CHAPTER 6

Seeing Your Romantic Future with Your Crystal Ball

Elyse's bronze skin glowed and her golden hair shimmered in the morning sunshine, a sight that made poor Dan feel as if the width of the dormitory cafeteria was as vast as the Red Sea. For the first three weeks of his freshman year, Dan had arrived at the cafeteria at 7:00 a.m. and had taken his seat by the west side bay windows with his plate of pancakes and sausage links. Elyse, the only other person in the cafeteria that early, arrived at 7:15 a.m. and took her seat in the sunshine of the east side windows, before striding to the middle of the room to prepare her breakfast plate at the salad bar. Dan found it odd that she chose to eat things like lettuce, garbanzo beans and beets for breakfast, but even her unusual dietary choices could not temper his growing infatuation.

The problem Dan faced is one that is familiar to most of us. How do you approach a complete stranger to whom you feel attracted, for no other reason than you like the look of him or her? As Dan sat there admiring Elyse from behind his tattered South Carolina baseball cap, he wondered if someone so beautiful and put together would ever want anything to do with a guy like him. Sometimes she received text messages, and her deep dimples would punctuate her perfect smile. Was she smiling because an equally perfect boyfriend was texting her? Was it a mundane text, but she smiled because she was always a ray of sunshine? That smile could have meant hundreds of things, could have been in response to hundreds of possibilities, which only illuminated the painful truth that Dan knew nothing about her. He needed to talk to her. So during the fourth week of his freshman year, Dan rose from his chair to get some salad.

That morning Elyse looked particularly well put together, with her polished dark brown leather boots, her light beige skirt, her neatly pressed, blue button-down and a delicate seashell bracelet. Dan arrived at the salad bar at the same time Elyse did and only then realized that his pancakes and sausage links occupied the entire face of his plate. With no turning back, Dan began putting items from the salad bar on top of his pancakes, slowly dying inside with the awkwardness of each garbanzo bean that rolled off the side of his plate. As the blue cheese dressing began dripping from the ladle he held, he felt a firm tug on his shirtsleeve and heard the jangle of seashells.

Elyse was taller than Dan had realized, about five-eleven, and as they now stood eye to eye, Dan tried to process that this moment was really happening. Trying to contain a rising giggle, Elyse let her index finger and thumb linger on Dan's shirtsleeve, her eyes bemused, before she whispered a rhetorical question "Why don't you bring your pancakes over to my table . . . ?"

A blissful series of weeks followed as Dan began dating the wonder that was Elyse Olsen. At some point Elyse initiated the "us talk," asking Dan, "So what's going on with us?" They resolved that they were in fact boyfriend and girlfriend, and that was when she asked him to dinner at her parents' house. Dan accepted the invitation and afterward returned to his room and had a panic attack. Sure, he had met the parents of his prom date, but he had never met the parents of someone he was seriously dating, and the task was made especially intimidating by the fact that Elyse's dad's first job out of college entailed spending three years as an offensive lineman in the National Football League.

Dan drove through the winding streets of a wealthy neighborhood a few miles outside of Boston, looking for the Olsens' home. He eventually saw their fortress, an enormous structure atop a steep hill. He parked at the base and gazed upward at the Olsens' medieval-looking abode, which was built of large gray stones and was guarded by gargoyles perched along the front. Before Dan began ascending the long winding staircase to the front door, he took a deep breath, straightened his tie and pulled his navy sports coat taut. As he drew closer, Dan felt his breathing accelerate, his chest constrict and his palms sweat. By the time he climbed the last step and stood in front of a door that looked like a drawbridge, Dan was on the verge of a panic attack. He should have pulled himself together before ringing the doorbell, but instead he mindlessly pushed the button, setting off a cascade of thundering bells.

The bells were still reverberating when Mr. Olsen's 290-pound frame fully occupied the doorway, and before he knew it, Dan was under the soaring arches of the long foyer, his clammy hand being crushed by Mr. Olsen's handshake. Mrs. Olsen was upon him almost simultaneously, lauding praise upon him in her jubilant voice and kissing him on the cheek. Elyse calmly emerged at the end of the foyer and looked at the scene with her bemused eyes. Then a brief palpable silence came over the foyer.

At the end of the foyer, a rumbling came from around the corner, and it sounded like a herd of galloping horses on the marble floor. Then El Capitan, the Olsen's freakishly large bullmastiff, burst onto the scene. El Capitan's size was more like that of a tiny pony than a dog, and he ran with such fervor that he was unable to make the ninety-degree pivot needed to turn toward the front door. After the beast crashed violently into the wall, he rotated his head in a spiral to shake off the blow, while a ring of snot and saliva made a halo around the black and brown fur of his head. Then, the mighty beast pivoted ninety degrees and fixed his gaze on Dan.

In human years, this two-year-old dog was about the age of a junior high boy. Recently, the Olsens had noticed that El Capitan had begun exploring his sexuality, which had led to indiscriminate exploration behaviors aimed at both animate and inanimate objects around the house. While El Capitan was galloping with such great enthusiasm and speed toward Dan, the Olsens were aware of how this was all adding up, but they were paralyzed for an instant by the absurdity of what was about to happen. Before anyone could stop the train wreck from unfolding, El Capitan had mounted Dan.

El Capitan did not mount Dan in typical fashion, which is to say around his shin or even his thigh. Instead, El Capitan was able to wrap his large, furry paws around Dan's shoulders. To Dan and those looking on in horror, this configuration seemed much more intimate. Dan could feel El Capitan's hot Purina breath, which was moist on his neck. The whole incident lasted just a few seconds, but those moments felt like an eternity to Dan, and during this time he saw his love life flash before his eyes.

It's funny, the memories your mind chooses to flash before your eyes. Among hundreds or thousands of possibilities, only a few scenes were needed to summarize Dan and Elyse's life together. In the end, it's the little things that are so telling. The way Elyse smiled effortlessly, strode confidently, dressed thoughtfully and tugged intently were manifestations of her core characteristics. There were things he loved, like her gregarious personality and self-confidence, but he also realized at that moment, for the first time, that Elyse was also a mean person. It sounded so childlike, calling someone mean, but there was no better way to explain why her teasing often crossed into biting criticism or why the glimmer in her eye at the sight of Dan's current misfortune was not indicative of amusement, but rather of some twisted sense of schadenfreude.

The complicated feelings that cascaded through his mind in that chaotic moment culminated in a strong hunch that there was something not quite right about Elyse. When Mr. Olsen eventually marched over and punted El Capitan into the wall, Dan was filled with a sense of urgency to figure out why he suddenly felt like he was standing in a den of lions.

LOOKING INTO YOUR CRYSTAL BALL

In our studies with people experiencing a breakup, participants often recall early warning signs of future relationship trouble, such as instances of insensitivity, cruelty or disinterest from their ex-partners. Although these warning signs are crystal clear with the benefit of hindsight, during the relationship people often ignore or rationalize them. When they summarize their reflections on these red flags, they often utter, with a tone of regret, an incomplete sentence that trails off. "I should have known..."

What exactly should they have known? What most people probably intend to say is, "I should have known...how things would end, based on the information that was unfolding about my partner." People stung by love lost might benefit from thinking that they should have known earlier in the last relationship where things were going, because that might encourage them to look for red flags and draw the appropriate conclusions from those red flags in the future. However, like many things in love, this is easier said than done.

Before coming to conclusions about why people have difficulty envisioning their romantic future, it's important to ask whether difficulty foreseeing an unhappy ending is usually due to a lack of motivation, a lack of ability or some combination of both. When it comes to motivation, people are often very motivated by the hope of finding enduring love, but they are less motivated to acknowledge that their current relationship is another dead end. So the motivation to envision the romantic future is often biased toward positive prognoses and against negative prognoses. Even if individuals are motivated to envision their romantic future, good or bad, researchers have found that they may be unable to predict their romantic future with accuracy. To consider how difficult it can be to envision the romantic future, consider the following analogy.

Imagine that a child asks you to help him or her complete a hundred-piece puzzle. Once you agree to lend a hand, the child dumps the puzzle pieces on the floor and informs you that he or she never found the top of the puzzle box, which has a picture of what the puzzle should look like when complete. The child has a vague recollection that the completed puzzle is of a lion or a tiger, but he or she is not sure which one. With one hundred puzzle pieces laid out randomly in front of you, the child asks, "What do you think it will be? A lion or a tiger?"

Your chances of guessing whether the puzzle is of a lion or a tiger are fifty-fifty, but given the number of pieces in the puzzle, you would be hard-pressed to achieve much better than 50 percent accuracy. If you had an infinite amount of time, then you could proceed with no strategy and no sense of urgency. Eventually, you would begin to see whether the puzzle was of a lion or a tiger, even before completing it, but if you had only fifteen minutes to complete it, then it would help to figure out as quickly as possible whether it was of a lion or a tiger. Once you knew what the end product was supposed to look like, the remaining pieces would fall more quickly into place. The best strategy for putting the pieces of the puzzle together in the most efficient and accurate way would be to:

1. Identify pieces that provide the most information (e.g., corners, an eye).

2. Put those key pieces in place first and then build around them.

3. Wait to make a decision about the outcome until enough pieces are in place.

What I'll explain in this chapter is a method for putting together the pieces of your love life with the purpose of predicting your romantic future. I'll begin by showing you why people have difficulty locating the most important traits in potential partners, how they make mistakes when predicting enduring love and why friends, family and even complete strangers are better at predicting a couple's fate than the two individuals actually involved in the relationship. Then I'll distill the results of hundreds of research papers to provide a manageable strategy, the equivalent of a crystal ball, to give you the best chance of finding enduring love. There are three main steps to accurately seeing your romantic future:

1. Accurately observe important traits during the early stages of dating.

2. Find a reliable framework that helps you organize those observations.

3. Use that framework to estimate the chances of forming a satisfying and stable relationship.

WHY WE MAKE BAD DECISIONS

When it comes to thinking about how to accurately identify the partners who are likley to provide enduring love, it's helpful to work from a framework that can simplify the task. Let's say that you are looking for partners who possess a positive trait, such as empathy. In the table below is a grid used in some studies of decision making that can help us understand good versus bad decisions. A relevant outcome can be present or absent, and people can say either that it is present (hit) or that it is not (miss).

	Respond Yes	Respond No
Trait Present	Hit	Miss
Trait Absent	False Alarm	Correct Rejection

This creates two possibilities for accurate judgments. A "hit" is when a trait is present and observers say, "Yes, a trait is present," and a "correct rejection" occurs when a trait is absent and observers say, "No, the trait is absent." If you went on two dates and Partner A is empathic and you identify Partner A as being empathic, then that would be a "hit" and if Partner B was not empathic and you deemed them unempathic then you would score a "correct rejection." There are also two ways to make mistakes. A "false alarm" occurs when observers think that a trait is present when it is actually absent, and a "miss" occurs when observers don't recognize the presence of a trait. You've probably witnessed friends caught in the haze of infatuation, mistakenly believing that they see desirable traits in their new partners (false alarms), such as empathy. Alternatively, friends can miss or deny the presence of negative traits in their partners, such as a tendency to be unempathic.

To think about this challenge from another angle, consider the decision to get a dog. When people are trying to decide which dog is right for them, they often make certain assumptions about the dog's abilities or personality. Take El Capitan, the bullmastiff who dry humped Dan in the foyer of the Olsens' home. Bullmastiffs tend to be very loyal and protective of their owners, and they are generally docile when given sufficient exercise. However, when not given the opportunity to blow off some steam outdoors, they can be like teenagers hyped up on sugar, testing the limits of the rules of the house. Chow chows look adorable, with their lush brown coats and pudgy faces. In China, where chow chows originated, they were selected for tasks such as hunting and guarding because of their traits, which include being very aggressive and unpredictable toward those who are not their owners. You might not want a bullmastiff if you live in a small apartment in New York City, and you might not select a chow chow as the dog for your children. These conclusions about which dogs to select are reached by knowing the dogs' traits, which allows you to predict their future behaviors and whether they are a good match for what you want.

Mistakenly assuming, based on its appearance, that the chow chow has a warm and cuddly personality would be an instance of a false alarm, and the consequences of this might be innocuous, with you feeling emotionally rejected by your own dog. However, missing the trait of aggressiveness in a chow chow could have catastrophic consequences. Similarly, mistakenly believing that a partner is warm or missing a partner's tendencies toward violence would have grave consequences for you and your future happiness and safety. Yet people often miss negative traits (insensitivity) and commit false positive errors (imagined empathy), which are errors in judgment that carry serious consequences for their future chances of having happy and stable relationships. So we need a framework that can focus us on the right things so that we can avoid missing important red flags or imagining traits that aren't really characteristic of a partner.

Paul Meehl was a legendary psychologist who was on the faculty at the University of Minnesota for over four decades and he was one of the first researchers to clearly show how errors in judgment occur. Professor Meehl had lost much of his eyesight, and his wife would sit alongside him in the audience at research talks, lovingly describing the tables and figures shown on the slides. From these verbal descriptions, Meehl probably reconstructed the tables and figures in his mind, and there was no one more capable of seeing through the "fuzzy thinking" of researchers who were trying to hide behind theoretical or methodological platitudes. His incisive mind probably helped him arrive at one of his most influential contributions in the 1970s, which was the finding that many psychologists were misdiagnosing their patients and choosing the wrong treatments for them.

The first thing to know about why people make bad decisions is that they make particularly poor predictions about big questions that require "yes or no" answers. Dozens of factors influence whether patients' medical conditions will be benign or fatal, whether countries will win a war or whether a couple's love will endure for decades. This inability to reliably predict big, complex outcomes is understandable because we are trying to decipher how dozens of factors will affect an outcome that has yet to occur. Thus, the first step to making better judgments is break down big "yes or no" decisions into smaller pieces, those pieces that we can observe right now.

The second thing to know is that many people often make mistakes when trying to assess even the smaller pieces of the relationship puzzle. Even experts make mistakes when they try to observe individuals' current levels of empathy, insensitivity or even violence. This means that in addition to breaking down complex relationship predictions into smaller pieces, we also need to figure out how to reliably assess traits that we can see right now.

The third thing to know is that even when people are given all the information about observable events or measurements, and therefore have the required ingredients to arrive at the correct decision, they can still make wrong decisions. Even when experts correctly measure the relevant factors and know how to prioritize and weight those factors, they can fall prey to biases or emotions that distort their predictions. So we need a systematic way to make sure our predictions are disciplined.

We've seen that predicting whether you will live happily ever after is complex, as it hinges on relationship satisfaction and relationship stability, which are themselves complex. Long-term relationship satisfaction and stability are considered complex outcomes because hundreds of factors influence whether couples remain satisfied and stable. In addition, these hundreds of influential factors interact over the course of thousands of days. However, we've seen that there is hope for correcting errors in judgment about potential partners and relationship outcomes, but it relies upon: (1) breaking big predictions into smaller pieces, (2) finding a method to accurately observe important pieces, and (3) following a disciplined system for using those pieces to predict relationship outcomes.

WHAT OTHER PEOPLE SEE THAT YOU DON'T SEE

One of the best examples of blind optimism regarding the long-term future of romantic relationships are people's answers when they are asked to estimate their likelihood of divorce. In one illustrative study, Blaine Flowers and his colleagues asked over one hundred married couples to estimate their likelihood of divorce. As discussed earlier, the Census Bureau's estimate of the divorce rate for the whole population is 50 percent, which is the most widely publicized number in the popular press. Despite this knowledge, participants in the study grossly underestimated the likelihood of their own divorce, with the average estimation of the likelihood of divorce hovering around 10 percent. Even when Flowers and his colleagues provided them with the actual divorce rate in a second study, just a few minutes before they wrote down their own chances of getting divorced, participants still underestimated their likelihood of divorce (23 percent). Participants also inflated their estimates of divorce risk for other couples (58 percent), probably to help rationalize away their gross underestimation of their own risk.

In another illuminating study of the positive illusions of couples in relationships, Chris Angew and his colleagues from Purdue University asked a group of dating couples and the couples' friends and family to rate the couples' degree of commitment, satisfaction and emotional investment. Agnew also asked the partners and friends/family to predict whether the couples would still be dating six months later or would break up. As seen in the following chart, the partners in the relationship made much more optimistic estimates regarding their degree of commitment, satisfaction and emotional investment in the relationship, compared to their friends and family.

Maybe positive illusions about relationship factors, such as commitment and emotional investment, do not matter if couples find what they are looking for: enduring love. So the real test would be whether the partners in the relationships or their friends/family would best predict whether the relationships stayed intact. At a six-month follow-up, Agnew and his colleagues contacted the partners to ask whether they were still dating. What they found was that friends and family were more accurate than the partners in the relationship themselves when it came to predicting whether the couple would be together or would have broken up.

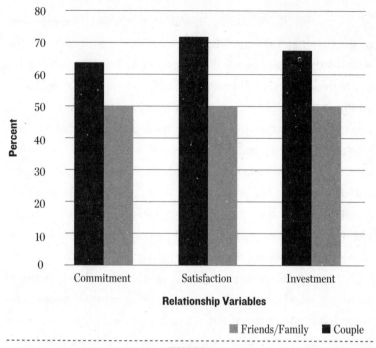

FIGURE 6.1

Differences between couples' evaluations of their relationships and friends'/
family evaluations of their relationships.

The seeds of a relationship's deterioration and partners' resentment are not seriously considered by most couples during their
early years of dating, even though just about everyone around the
couple can see the looming conflict and the instability with great
clarity. There are multiple lines of converging evidence to suggest
that people can anticipate the fate of a romantic relationship with
a great deal of accuracy before a couple ever marries.

John Gottman and his colleagues from the University of
Washington and the Gottman Institute have conducted a series
of studies that are focused on predicting divorce based on brief
observations of newlyweds interacting. In the typical Gottman
study, couples come to the laboratory and are asked to talk to

each other for fifteen minutes about a "continuing disagreement" or the "events of the day." Researchers, who have never met the couples they are observing on video, code the interactions for key behaviors, such as instances of defensiveness or resentment and problem-solving strategies. Numerous studies suggest that these small glimpses into couples' lives, lasting only fifteen minutes and entailing conversational subjects as mundane as "events of the day," allow researchers to predict whether those couples will divorce fourteen years later with about 90 percent accuracy. So total strangers armed with a coding system and fifteen minutes of video can predict with a fair degree of accuracy whether you will be divorced or will still be married to your partner years later.

Although the predictive power exhibited in these studies is stunning, who has the time to be trained in complex coding systems that require expertise in the coding of facial expressions, the interpretation of physiological data and a host of other skills often learned during years of doctoral training? Robert Waldinger and his colleagues at Harvard Medical School and Judge Baker Children's Center conducted a clever study asking a simple question, "Could psychology undergraduates with no formal training somehow pick up on couples' behaviors accurately enough to predict divorce?" They were very able. In fact, untrained undergraduates observed couples interact for ten minutes on video, and their observations were used to predict which couples would divorce five years later with 81 percent accuracy. Thus, even total strangers with no formal training can make more accurate predictions of divorce probability than partners who have spent thousands of hours with each other. What is it that other people notice about couples' relationships that the couples themselves can't see?

There are dozens of other studies demonstrating that partners in relationships are relatively poor judges when it comes to predicting big relationship outcomes for themselves, such as whether they have found "the one" who will bring them long-term relationship satisfaction and stability. Underlying this inaccuracy is the fact that, as in diagnosing complex diseases or determining whether a war can be won, judging whether complex romantic relationships will be stable is a "yes or no" decision about a complex outcome.

WHAT SHOULD I BE LOOKING FOR IN A PARTNER?

You should look for traits. *Traits* can be broadly defined as "characteristics or dispositions that are consistent or stable over time." There's a broad range of factors that qualify as traits, including values, personality characteristics, abilities and physical features. What all of these have in common is that they tend to remain constant for years or even a lifetime. Important traits of potential partners can be accurately observed during the early stages of dating, and accurately assessing potential partners' traits can help improve how well you predict relationship satisfaction and stability.

One reason that traits are worthy of our attention early in the dating process is that they don't change much across the life span. So the benefit of correctly identifying desirable traits and judging correctly when bad traits are truly absent (correct rejections) ends up being multiplied for years. Similarly, the costs of bad decisions, such as rejecting perfectly good partners based on false alarms or missing a great partner, are also multiplied for many years to come. It's like making a good decision when you buy an umbrella. Your one-time decision to buy a good umbrella or a bad umbrella will make you feel fortunate or remorseful, respectively, every single time it rains.

Psychological traits, such as personality, values and interests, are heritable, show stability from childhood to adolescence and become even more stable once people reach young adulthood. Children who are generous and calm tend to become generous and calm teens. Young adults who are mean and insensitive tend to be mean and insensitive senior citizens. Both desirable and undesirable traits become well entrenched by a combination of individuals' genetic dispositions, their rearing environments as children and the environments they freely select for themselves as teens and young adults.

So one reason to look for traits in potential partners is that they are very stable over time. If you choose someone with traits that drive you crazy or make you sad while you're dating, then those traits will make you crazy or sad for decades to come. So you want to choose well, because what you see is what you get.

Another good reason to focus on traits is that they can be observed with accuracy, and psychologists have developed frameworks for helping you organize traits in ways that provide meaningful insights about potential partners. Traits are predictive of highly consequential outcomes in life, and so the bounty or bane of partners' traits will multiply across the years of a relationship. Researchers who assess participants' traits in adolescence or young adulthood are able to predict outcomes decades later, including their levels of happiness with life, their physical health, psychopathology, occupational success, criminality and, of course, their romantic relationship outcomes.

Thus traits are powerful predictors of future outcomes, but there are so many traits that we need some frameworks to make our observations meaningful.

PUTTING THE PIECES TOGETHER TO SEE YOUR FUTURE

Once you carefully assess traits, then you need to put those pieces together into a coherent framework to predict your romantic future.

Three Frameworks for Your Three Wishes

One of the first psychologists to ambitiously study traits was Gordon Allport, who was working as a psychology professor at Harvard University in the early 1900s. He began his investigation by sifting through his dictionary, from cover to cover, for words that could be considered "traits." If you think about the words we use to describe the diverse array of people we meet, then it makes sense that there is a need for linguistic nuances when describing "who somebody is" or "who you are." Allport found over four thousand words that could refer to personality traits alone. In the table below are five categories of traits, and a few examples are given for each to help us begin to think about the overwhelming number of words that could be used to describe potential partners' traits.

Family	Values	Personality	Ability	Attractiveness
Parenting	Altruistic	Extroversion	Artistic	Face
Parental Divorce	Power	Openness	Athletic	Height
Attachment	Autonomy	Agreeableness	Mathematical	Weight
Siblings	Conformity	Conscientiousness	Social Skills	Facial Symmetry
Approval	Stimulation	Neuroticism	Common Sense	Skin Tone

Of course, we could add many more traits, such as "religion," and all the religious denominations, or "child rearing," and the hundreds of parenting styles and parenting behaviors. It's easy to see that there are thousands of possible traits, but the problem is that singles get only three wishes when it comes to choosing desirable traits in their romantic partners. So we need a way to whittle down these thousands of possibilities to a workable number of traits and then to organize those traits in a framework that can be used to make meaningful predictions.

If you can accurately decipher key traits in potential partners, then you have the opportunity to take advantage of research findings that demonstrate how certain traits predict marital outcomes. I've selected three frameworks that are elegantly simple ways to organize our thinking about three wishes for traits in the search for a great partner: personality traits, attachment styles and relationship markers.

Personality Traits

Personality traits describe how people tend to respond across situations. When someone asks, "What's she like?" people often answer by citing personality traits. They'll say someone is extroverted or introverted, nice or mean, calm or neurotic. These descriptors tell us something about how people usually think and act across a variety of situations. For example, extroverted people are usually talkative at home, with friends and at work. Emotionally stable people are calm when things are going well, but also in the midst of a crisis.

Personality traits are highly heritable, moderately stable in childhood and adolescence, and very stable in adulthood. Personality traits begin to show themselves early in infancy, and so infants' tendencies to be calm, easily frightened or fussy are easily noted. We can think of personality as something that is generally "in place" by the time we meet potential partners in young adulthood. Luckily, personality traits can be decoded accurately by using the proper set of methods, and these traits are powerful predictors of whether partners are likely to provide satisfying and stable relationships.

Attachment Styles

Environmental forces influence even highly heritable psychological traits, such as personality. Dispositions can be enhanced or diminished by how caregivers choose to respond to their infants' physical and emotional needs. An infant born with a genetic predisposition to be extroverted can have that tendency enhanced by parents who respond to their child's talkative nature by being talkative and engaging. Conversely, parents who are introverted or are unresponsive might diminish their child's extroversion. Similarly, a child born with emotionally unstable genetic tendencies could have this genetic risk made worse by unpredictable or harsh parenting. Conversely, parents who are consistent and calm might mitigate a child's risk of reaching their full potential to be emotionally unstable.

The ways that children and parents interact culminate in children's "attachment" to their parents, which could be secure or insecure depending on the quality of the caregiving relationship. Parents who are responsive and loving and provide a sense of safety tend to have children who grow up to believe that others can be relied upon and who have the confidence to form healthy, loving relationships beyond those with their caregivers. Attachment styles can be rated and measured with accuracy using a variety of methods and observations. Similar to personality traits, knowing whether a partner is securely or insecurely attached gives you a powerful way to predict whether he or she is likely to provide a satisfying and stable relationship in the future.

Relationship Markers

Once we account for someone's personality traits and the parenting environment in which he or she was raised, the icing on the cake is observing how the person acts within a current romantic relationship. Although red flags that occur when you first start dating someone are not traditionally thought of as traits, partners do show great consistency in how they think, act and feel in close relationships. As often happens in early dating relationships, there are certain things your partner does that can give you pause. It's hard to know whether your partner's behaviors that raise red flags are warning signs of worse things to come or just your idiosyncratic worry about something that is probably irrelevant.

It would be nice if there were reliable research findings about which of the hundreds of relationship behaviors that take place over the course of a relationship are significant signs of future relationship dysfunction. The three relationship markers we'll review include: (1) how partners think about the cause of relationship problems, (2) how partners ask for what they want and (3) how partners magnify positive aspects of the relationship.

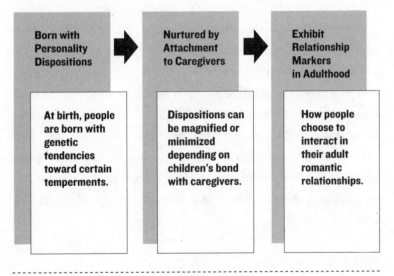

FIGURE 6.2

An overview of three key frameworks for making informed wishes.

Knowing how to assess partners using these three frameworks—namely, personality traits, relational history through attachment and current relationship markers for dysfunction—gives you three different opportunities to think about making your three wishes for traits in a partner. You can think of these three frameworks as key pieces of the relational puzzle, which provide you with the best chance to see what the puzzle will look like in the end. If it's difficult to assess a partner's attachment to his or her caregivers, then your three wishes could be based on three key personality traits. If you're having a hard time getting a read on personality or attachment, then you could examine key relationship markers in your dating relationship with your partner. Although you will end up with more than three wishes for traits after we cover these three frameworks, wishing for anything based on these three frameworks can improve your odds of finding happily ever after.

DO ENGAGEMENTS, MARRIAGES OR BABIES CHANGE PEOPLE?

No. Researchers who study how to help distressed couples through psychotherapy are increasingly coming to the humbling conclusion that some distressed couples appear to be treatment resistant. In other words, the best couples' therapies available don't work for some couples. Psychologists have scurried to find out why, and one plausible explanation is that some treatment-resistant couples may have had in place many individual risk factors for destructive conflict or instability before they ever met their current partner. This means that the seeds of discord and divorce would have been evident in the traits of each partner from the day they met.

So a third reason to look for traits in potential partners is that frameworks used to organize traits allow you to make stronger predictions about the future of your relationship. Consider the following example to contemplate what happens when children are given genetic predispositions by their parents and then are raised by those same parents who exhibit those traits. Imagine that Dan has a genetic predisposition toward anxiety and is raised by his biological parents, who are both anxious people. In infancy, Dan is more likely than other infants to become easily upset and to scare easily in the presence of strangers, and he is less likely than most infants to explore his surroundings.

Imagine the differences in how an anxious parent and a calm parent would respond to baby Dan crying. The calm parent might exhibit calm body language, use a tone of voice that is reassuring and allow the infant some space before intervening. An anxious parent would be more likely to startle the infant, use an intense, semi-panicked tone of voice and smother the infant with cloying attention. The well-intended actions of the anxious parent make the infant more nervous and contribute to the creation in the infant of a mental map of anxiety: when something feels scary or nerve-racking, you escalate the emotional response to the situation.

What happens over thousands of interactions spread over many years is that children's genetic tendencies toward traits are made more pronounced and stable by parents who exhibit those traits. This is not always a negative phenomenon, because if you are born to happy and kind parents, then your tendency toward these dispositions can become more pronounced by your environment. The implication for our purposes here is that if a romantic partner was born to happy and kind parents, then those parents might have strengthened these tendencies in their child through the models they provided him or her for responding to various interpersonal situations.

As children mature and are given and seek more freedom, they can more easily choose their own influences outside of their parents' home. Although teens and adults sometimes try wildly different activities, they tend to select environments that are congruent with their existing traits and home environment. For example, introverts may choose to ask a high school friend to coffee on Friday night, whereas extroverts may call ten friends and ask them to go mingle at a party with a bunch of strangers. So if you were to take a snapshot of an introvert on a Friday night, you would see him or her having a quiet conversation with one other person in the soft light of a coffee shop, whereas in another snapshot, you would see the extrovert screaming at the top of his or her lungs under the strobe lights of a nightclub. The introvert is exhibiting introverted behavior, and the extrovert is exhibiting extroverted behavior, but that's partly because they have selected environments that enhance their traits. After thousands of Friday nights of choosing different environments, the introvert and the extrovert have created a lifestyle that stabilizes their traits, because those environments "pull for" those traits.

Even when teens and young adults don't have the luxury of choosing their environments, they still find avenues to shape their environments in ways that are congruent with their traits. For example, if an extrovert and an introvert were both thrown into a party with a bunch of strangers, the introvert would be more likely to ask other people closed-ended "yes or no" questions, whereas the extrovert would try to keep conversations going with more open-ended questions and would ask more follow-up questions than the introvert. Developmental psychologists say that people's traits "evoke," or "pull for," certain responses from the environments they choose.

We can see why traits become so stable and predictive of future behaviors. We inherit certain genetic tendencies toward certain traits from our parents, and when we are raised by our biological parents with those same traits, those inherent traits are modeled and reinforced. When teens and young adults have the freedom to choose their own paths, they tend to selectively choose environments that are congruent with their dispositions, further enhancing the stability of their traits.

All this talk about traits being stable does not presuppose an inherently negatively view of the human condition. Saying that traits are stable is taking a neutral stance, because it does not favor positive or negative traits. If you choose some dreamy partner who is bright, funny, self-confident, kind and good-looking, and loves his or her mother, then the good news is that when you reassess your romantic situation after twenty-five years of marriage, that partner, compared to others in your same age cohort, will probably still be bright, funny, self-confident, kind and good-looking, and a good son or daughter.

In the end, you will have a list of more than three traits to wish for, but all the traits I will be recommending are known to be important predictors of relationship satisfaction and relationship stability. In the coming chapters, I'll review methods for getting an accurate read on a potential partner's traits, even if you're lost in the haze of infatuation, so that you can then determine early on in the relationship whether he or she possesses the personality, attachment style and relationship markers that are right for you. Although it's difficult to discover whether a partner has too many traits working against him or her, it's even more difficult to realize this when you're married with two kids and a mortgage, and that's why smart singles choose to approach relationship decisions with intelligence and discipline.

WHAT YOU SEE IN A PARTNER IS WHAT YOU GET. FOREVER.

In the midst of the horror that was El Capitan mounting him in the Olsens' foyer, as Dan's romantic life was flashing before his eyes, he realized that he had never had occasion to smile at breakfast, he replayed how reluctant he had been to walk to the salad bar that day and he recalled his inability to respond confidently when Elyse tugged on his shirt. As all these vivid scenes whirled around in his mind, Dan realized that Elyse was the kind of woman he hoped to marry one day and that Elyse would never marry a guy like him.

Although Dan possessed some traits that worked against him, he was gifted with crystal clear insight about how people functioned. He knew that he was far less confident, emotionally stable and ambitious in his work than Elyse. She also had certain liabilities in her constellation of traits, but those were not deal breakers for him. However, he knew that his trait liabilities would eventually be deal breakers for Elyse. A few months later he would prove to be right.

To Dan's credit, he recognized his limitations and then pushed himself beyond what was comfortable for him. He forced himself to walk up to the salad bar, even if he was rendered inept when faced with actually interacting. Elyse was disposed to be and was raised to be more extroverted and confident, and she possessed great social skills, so she was easily and effectively able to take command of their initial encounter. Dan began to have a premonition even before that fateful night at the Olsens' home that Elyse would need someone who could consistently take charge of life. That wasn't Dan.

After Mr. Olsen punted El Capitan into the wall, the beast shook it off and galloped away, disappearing down the long foyer and out of sight. Dan continued to stand there, immobilized, like a deer in headlights, his tie and sports coat disheveled, his face flushed bright red, and El Capitan's saliva glistening on his neck. After a bit, Elyse broke the stunned silence and elicited relieved collective laughter when she observed, "El Capitan must really like you. . . ."

In the vast dining room, with its vaulted ceilings and large chandelier, Dan sat down across from Mr. Olsen and found himself flanked by the two Olsen women at a surprisingly small square table. El Capitan now lay serenely in the corner of the dining room, watching a calm settle over Dan as the evening began to take a turn for the better. The Olsens were excellent conversationalists and quickly zeroed in on Dan's passion for his philosophy coursework and gaming. He felt at ease speaking about academic topics, and his dry sense of humor began to blossom in the company of this bright, enthusiastic family.

After the Olsens and Dan had had a glass or two of wine, the comedy at the table turned into slapstick and the laughter became uproarious. Dan was fully participating in the volley and gladly took his turn adding to the hilarity. Dan's trait-like anxiety was diluted by the merlot, and he now felt so comfortable that he looked to his right after Mrs. Olsen had said something particularly funny, and went to give her a "You're funny" pat on the shoulder. Regrettably, right at the moment when Dan's hand was irretrievably set in motion, Mrs. Olsen rotated forty-five degrees toward Dan to add a follow-up quip. The scene unraveled in slow motion, as everyone at the table witnessed Dan's open-palmed right hand land squarely on Mrs. Olsen's ample left breast.

I don't think El Capitan's dry humping, or even Dan's inadvertent groping of Mrs. Olsen, led Elyse to break up with him a few months later. Dan's difficulty handling those situations deeply troubled Elyse, and Dan was deeply hurt by Elyse's cruelty after that disastrous night. While she wondered what would happen when bigger stresses occurred in the future, he wondered what would happen when they faced more important issues in the future and whether she would handle his personal shortcomings with such derision. How would Dan and Elyse respond to chronic duress at work, to the tough stresses of raising children, or to one of them falling ill? If she could barely stand his passivity and he was emotionally destroyed by her insensitivity at this juncture in their relationship, how could they possibly handle more interpersonally complicated challenges?

What is difficult about love stories like Dan and Elyse's is that partners usually don't possess uniformly good or bad traits. People often possess some good traits, such as being smart and funny, and these are often mixed with undesirable traits, such as emotional instability and low self-confidence. Thus, singles are faced with the challenge of assessing the overall value of potential partners through weighting their positive and negative traits.

Wouldn't it be nice if singles who were trying to assess whether they could live happily ever after with a potential partner knew whether the benefits associated with self-confidence outweighed the costs associated with neuroticism? Wouldn't it be nice if singles could look at a summary of research findings to assess whether Partner A's high self-confidence is worth more than Partner B's kindness? It certainly would be nice if you had some general sense of how to weight the benefits and costs of key traits, because then you would be on the road to making more informed decisions about potential partners.

I just might have something so nice.

CHAPTER 7

The Power of Personality

One of the best love stories I have ever heard was told to me when I was ten years old. It was a spring morning on the porch of my godparents' home when Ethan and Catherine told me the fairy-tale story of how they had met over fifty years ago. They met in the late 1940s, during one of the most significant high school football games the state had ever witnessed. Ethan was the starting quarterback for a scrappy bunch of guys from a tough part of town, and he had led his West High team to an undefeated season. Their opponent was a traditional football powerhouse that was led by a star linebacker named Lars Stevenson. As a senior in high school, Ethan was about five-ten, and he recalled weighing a rail-thin 150 pounds. He was handsome and fast afoot, and beneath his bowl-cut brown hair was a lightning-fast mind. Lars was a two-hundred-pound block of muscle, known for his bruising hits in East High's painfully simple but awesome defense, which minimized the need for Lars to think and maximized the possibility for him to punish opposing offenses.

On the sidelines, Catherine was the head cheerleader for East High, and she led her squad in front of a sold-out crowd watching a tightly fought contest between two great teams piloted by two great players. West High's best play was an option, which maximized Ethan's speed as he raced toward the sidelines, trying to get the corner, but often created an intriguing matchup between his speed and Lars's power. During the third quarter and down by ten points, West High ran an option toward the side of the field occupied by the East High players, cheerleaders and fans. After Ethan's tight end missed his block on Lars, Lars was left with a clear shot as Ethan rounded the corner, and with his full force, he sent Ethan flying out of bounds headfirst like a bullet. Ethan had so much momentum from Lars's hit that he flew right past the players and coaches standing on the sideline. Catherine and her cheerleading squad were facing the fans in the stands and thus were unaware that Ethan was bulleting toward them.

When Ethan's leather helmet hit the back side of Catherine's calves, the force of the blow sent her into a series of pike twists in the air. Ethan eventually screeched to a halt on the dirt track and lay unconscious on his back. As fate would have it, Catherine fell from her twists face-first and found herself perfectly aligned with Ethan's face. Catherine was very proper as a godmother, even compared to other godmother-aged people I knew as a boy, so I could infer that she must have been fairly proper as a young girl. Yet she reported to me that as she lay atop Ethan and stared into what she imagined would be his eyes were he not unconscious, it never occurred to her to stand up. In the few seconds that elapsed between the time Ethan and Catherine collided and the moment the people on the sideline realized what had happened and responded, Ethan's eyes fluttered open, and he told me on the porch that he had never seen someone so lovely. In those few seconds before the coaches and other concerned adults arrived to pick up Catherine and examine Ethan, their attention shifted from the task of winning the most important football game in decades.

Catherine returned to cheering and Ethan returned to quarterbacking, but in the midst of the most important game of their lives, the only thing on both their minds was each other. So Ethan led his team back in the third and fourth quarters, partly due to his love of the game and his team, but mostly because he was a boy trying to impress a pretty cheerleader. The frenzied crowd might have thought that the peak of the drama was when Ethan's West High team faced a third down with just a few seconds to go and needed eight yards for the winning touchdown, and Ethan raced around the corner on an option and, in a show of superhuman strength, stiff-armed Lars for a good three yards to get into the end zone and deliver the state championship to his team. Catherine almost jumped for joy at the sight of Ethan's late-game heroics.

After the game, the real drama was about to begin. The West High players put their coach and Ethan on their shoulders and carried them off the field, while Ethan's quick mind immediately shifted toward his predicament with Catherine. In an age without Facebook or Google searching, one needed to be assertive when face-to-face romantic opportunities arose, and so Ethan knew that he needed to establish a connection immediately, as Catherine lived over an hour away by car. He deployed his offensive linemen to quickly gather intelligence about Catherine, and they reported that she was currently consoling the girls on her squad, who were crestfallen by the loss. They found out that she also had a boyfriend—Lars.

While both teams showered and changed into their street clothes, Ethan covertly sent two of the younger players to the parking lot, where one of them, the son of the local mechanic, jimmied open the hood to

Lars's car and removed a few parts essential for ignition. So when Lars and Catherine eventually got into Lars's car and he turned the key in the ignition, they heard the sputtering sound of a car unable to start. At that very moment, Ethan pulled alongside in his dilapidated Chevy and motioned to Catherine to roll down her window. As a ten-year-old boy, I was stunned to hear about all this mischievous activity from my seventy-year-old godfather, and even more stunned to hear about what he said to Catherine, who still sat in Lars's car. "You want to go for a soda?"

Without a moment of hesitation, Catherine jumped out of Lars's car and into Ethan's life. At the local soda fountain that evening, Ethan and Catherine sat side by side, sharing a milkshake with two straws. The whole moment seemed so ideal in my ten-year-old mind, like a Norman Rockwell scene come to life, so it seemed that there was one question left to ask Grandpa Ethan:

"Did you ask Grandma Catherine to marry you that night?"

"Now, that would have been bold! But no, not that night."

"Why not?"

"You need some time to find out who a girl really is."

"Didn't you know Grandma Catherine after the soda shop?"

"I knew there was something special about her. Not sure how I knew... but I knew."

Psychologists now know how Grandpa Ethan and others have a "hunch" about new romantic interests. In this chapter, I'll show you how dramatic advances in personality research can help you decode the personality traits of potential partners and forecast whether they're likely to provide a relationship as happy and as enduring as Ethan and Catherine's marriage.

WHAT IS PERSONALITY, AND WHERE DO I GET ONE?

We've already established that personality is "who you are." Personality traits describe how you generally think, act and feel across most situations. Although some people might be more talkative in one-on-one situations versus large groups, or others might feel neurotic on planes but not in cars, when someone strongly possesses a personality trait, you can usually predict his or her responses across many different scenarios. So personality is more often than not who you are across a variety of situations.

Your personality comes from a combination of genetics, early childhood experiences and the environments you chose to place yourself in during adolescence and adulthood. As infants' genes are laying the map for how tall they grow or how quickly they begin to talk, their genes are also laying a map for how their brain develops and functions, which influences how they respond psychologically to their environments. Early in infancy, humans exhibit consistent responses across situations, and these temperaments help account for why some babies always cry when held by a stranger or tend to maintain long gazes when novel people or toys are introduced to them.

Infant temperaments show moderate predictive power of childhood and adult personality, and so babies that easily cry tend to be fearful adults, and babies that smile to engage adults in social smiling tend to be extroverted as adults. Once people reach adolescence and adulthood, their personalities lead them to freely seek out environments that are congruent with their traits. So the extrovert goes to parties, and the novelty seeker joins the extreme sports club at school.

One of the methods researchers use to study how much "nature and nurture" influence various traits are twin studies. Consider the following hypothetical example: Identical twins Laura and Abbey are born to a biological mother and father who are both extroverted, giving them a genetic tendency toward extroversion. At birth, they are separated and adopted into two different homes. If extroverted parents adopt Laura and introverted parents adopt Abbey, then the question becomes one of nature and nurture. When they are adults, will Laura and Abbey resemble more their adoptive parents or their biological parents on the extroversion-introversion continuum? These identical twins share 100 percent of their genes, but they do not share the same parenting environment, which provides a great test of how "nature" and "nurture" interact when it comes to traits.

The results of many twin studies comparing twins reared apart and twins reared together have demonstrated that identical twins tend to resemble their biological parents more than their adoptive parents on a number of psychological traits. This is not to say that the adoptive parents have no influence; it simply implies that what the twins inherited genetically from their biological parents still has an influence on their traits.

You've probably seen examples in the press of identical twins separated at birth and reunited as adults who have married women by the same name, given their dogs the same name and happen to both like Pepsi instead of Coke. Although some of these similarities are mere coincidence, at the abstract level of personality traits or abilities, a number of studies have demonstrated that many traits are partly heritable. In a 2004 article, behavioral geneticist Tom Bouchard summarized the heritability of various traits, and he found in his review that some traits are highly heritable, such as extroversion, whereas others show relatively lower rates of heritability, such as a tendency toward being religious.

Traits	Heritability
Intelligence	50–82%
Height	70–95%
Extroversion	54%
Emotional Stability	48%
Agreeableness	42%
Religiousness	30–35%

However, genes are far from the whole story when it comes to how traits develop. Familial environments and environments outside of the family can enhance or curb genetic tendencies. Familial environments include the influence of parents and siblings or other family members living under the same roof. We'll examine parent-child relationships in great depth in the next chapter, but for now it's important to consider the following phenomenon: children inherit their biological parents' genetic tendencies (e.g., extroversion) at birth, and then their parents display those same traits while raising their children (e.g., being talkative)?

For example, if both parents are high in extroversion, they likely pass along genetic tendencies to their children that dispose the children to act in a more social manner. Extroverted parents are more likely to respond enthusiastically and talkatively to infants, which in turn shapes the child's beliefs about how to interact with others. Infants prone to extroversion also tend to engage in more eye contact with people other than their parents, which tends to elicit reciprocated attention, thereby positively reinforcing the infant's social behavior.

In early adolescence, teens increasingly begin to seek out nonfamilial environments that are consistent with their personalities and that enhance their personalities. For example, extroverts choose to go party with hundreds of people instead of going to a movie with one person, and teens high in openness seek excitement through healthy extracurricular activities or, alternatively, through risky sexual or drug use behaviors. Once they are situated in these environmental niches, their personality dispositions are left to flourish. The extrovert mingles and looks extroverted while talking up a storm. The novelty seeker looks wild and crazy while bungee jumping or doing a line of cocaine off the toilet seat. The tendency for people with strong traits to "evoke" reactions from their environments further stabilizes their personality.

However, children's genetic tendencies toward certain dispositions, whether those dispositions are desirable or undesirable traits, can be enhanced or diminished by the attachment bonds they form with their caregivers. We saw that children with a secure attachment to their caregivers are confident that they will be loved, nurtured and treated in a consistent manner, whereas avoidant and anxious children struggle with being able to rely upon their caregivers in times of need.

Do these findings regarding the stability of traits mean that people can't change? In ongoing relationships, the findings regarding the stability of traits can be twisted into a perverse excuse for behaving badly, such as when the guilty partner declares, "I can't help it. It's just who I am...." I'm not a big fan of the word *can't,* particularly when the well-being of others is involved. Oftentimes, it would be more accurate if the guilty party declared, "I can help it, but it's difficult for me..."

For example, Catherine might typically be engaging and gregarious, averaging thirty minutes of talking per hour spent with Ethan. On a given night she speaks for only five minutes per hour. Ethan might think that this is a sign that the relationship is going sour or that she's losing her sociability, but the odds are that the next night she'll be right back at her average of thirty minutes per hour. Ethan might average only ten minutes of talking per hour, but on the night he meets Catherine's parents for the first time, he might be mindful of acting more extroverted and push beyond his normal range up to fifteen minutes per hour. That one instance does not make him an extrovert; rather it's just a case of an introverted person being self-aware and selectively pushing himself into behaviors that are needed in a given situation.

So people can be a little bit more extroverted, a little happier or a little more at peace with who they are. People don't really change, but they can become more aware of how they typically respond to situations and can push themselves to alter their natural responses. The fact remains that when it comes to choosing a romantic partner, what you see is what you get. Forever. Although this second type of change is possible, why would you go into a marriage relying only upon a partner's willingness to manage their negative traits, rather than choose someone from the start who gives your relationship the best chance of success? Partners who give your relationship the best chance of success also tend to be the kind of people who are most likely to manage whatever weaknesses they have with maturity. So, once again, finding happily ever after begins with choosing someone with the right traits. Once you know the facts and the data, it makes it harder to avoid being honest with yourself about which partners possess the right traits for you, but overriding your old partner selection tendencies is far more difficult to achieve.

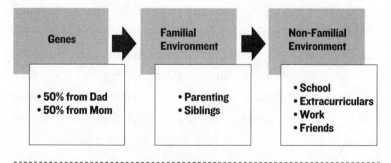

FIGURE 7.1
Genetic and environmental influences on personality development.

Not all personality theories and measures are created equal. In fact, many of the personality inventories that are widely used are of dubious quality. A good measure of personality should: (1) assess a manageable number of personality traits, (2) provide a relatively thorough and accurate description of someone, (3) include traits that are stable over time and (4) accurately predict a range of important outcomes. There are very few theories that meet all four criteria, and some theories include three core personality traits, but one theory that has received strong empirical support is the Big Five model of personality, which includes the five broad traits listed in the table below.

Personality Trait	Subscales
Openness to Experience	Spontaneous, impulsive, seeks novel experiences
Conscientiousness	Organized, motivated, achievement striving, disciplined
Extroversion	Talkative, energetic, gregarious, assertive
Agreeableness	Warm, kind, empathic, altruistic, modest
Neuroticism	Moody, irritable, anxious, depressed

Assessing Personality with Accuracy

Personality can be easily measured by providing individuals with well-studied personality scales that are known to be reliable and accurate and having them self-report on their levels of personality traits. The advantage of self-report methods of personality assessment is that people have unique insight into what is happening internally in terms of their thoughts, emotions and preferences.

However, in matters of love, people are often motivated to distort the self-assessments either to protect their self-esteem or to hide less than desirable characteristics from you. There are many methods for assessing personality. We'll examine in particular the accuracy of self-reports, your chances of accurately rating a partner's personality (partner reports) and what happens when people outside of the relationship, such as friends and family, provide ratings (ratings of friends and family). You can think about getting these ratings through diverse means as a way to triangulate around what a partner's personality is really like.

Self-Reports

One of the most straightforward and convenient ways to assess personality is to ask people to rate themselves on a self-report scale. Part of the thinking with self-report scales of personality is that there is no one who can report on traits better than the person who spends the most time with the self, which is the self. Only you have access to your every inner thought, feeling and behavior across many situations. I've included an example of a brief measure developed by William Swann and his colleagues at the University of Texas, which provides relatively good accuracy and reliability when measuring the Big Five personality traits.

Although self-report can be an accurate method for assessing personality, it operates under the assumption that the individual has a low motivation to skew the results. For example, if a personality inventory is being given as part of a custody battle in a divorce case, is administered as part of a job interview or, let's say, is given to people invested in perpetuating a romantic relationship, then respondents will likely be motivated to "look good" or "socially desirable," which leads to less accurate results. Similarly, potential partners who are vying for your favor might be motivated to inflate their good traits and minimize their bad traits.

Indicate the extent to which you agree or disagree with each item. You should rate the extent to which the traits apply to you, even if one charactersitic applies more strongly than the other.

Disagree Strongly	Disagree Moderately	Disagree a Little	Neither Agree or Not Agree	Agree a Little	Agree Moderately	Agree Strongly
1	2	3	4	5	6	7

I see myself as:

1. _____ Extroverted, enthusiastic
2. _____ Critical, quarrelsome
3. _____ Dependable, self-disciplined
4. _____ Anxious, easily upset
5. _____ Open to new experiences, complex
6. _____ Reserved, quiet
7. _____ Sympathetic, warm
8. _____ Disorganized, careless
9. _____ Calm, emotionally stable
10. _____ Conventional, uncreative

Note: Go to www.tytashiro.com to score and see how you compare to other people.

Partner Reports

If new partners cannot be trusted to provide accurate reports of their personality, then maybe you can accurately decode the levels of potential partners' traits. Garth Fletch and Patrick Kerr were at the University of Canterbury when they analyzed the results of forty-eight studies that focused on the accuracy and bias involved with partner's perceptions of each other. What they found was that partners in romantic relationships, just like one might expect of someone self-reporting, significantly inflated their judgments of their partner's traits and of their relationships. People rate their partners more favorably than their partners rate themselves, and people rate their partners as significantly more attractive than outside observers do. These "positive illusions" of their relationship quality and their partner's positive traits were largely exaggerated early in the relationship, but they steadily diminished over decades of marriage, as the glossy veneer of passionate love faded.

Researchers have begun to show just how infatuation clouds our judgment during the early stages of relationships. Given that a relationship might entail sacrificing time, career opportunities and emotional energy, we need to believe that those efforts are worthwhile, that we are with someone who is worthwhile. When couples are faced with justifying the tremendous sacrifice of time and energy that goes into committed relationships, researchers find that couples are more than willing to inflate their partner's positive traits and minimize their negative traits. So it appears that even the best of us would be wise not to rely solely upon our informal estimations of a partner's traits.

Ratings of Friends and Family

Here's one of the most difficult facts to stomach when it comes to accurate ratings of personality in romantic situations, which is that on average, your friends and even your family know best. A number of cleverly designed studies have asked partners in romantic relationships and their friends or family about the couple's degree of love and commitment, and the likelihood that their relationship will endure months later or even culminate in marriage. Across these studies, partners in the relationship report inflated views of the degree of love and commitment in the relationship compared to the ratings from friends or family. Furthermore, the partners overestimate the probability that the relationship will endure, compared to their friends and family. Thus, it is no surprise that we have all seen situations in which everybody knows that a friend's relationship is a complete disaster, except for the friend in the relationship. Whether it is a friend or a family member, these data point toward the same question, what is it that they see that you do not?

The answer is twofold. They accurately discern stable traits about each partner from observing speech, body language and other clues, which help them understand things about the person now and how the person will likely think and behave in the future. Second, the observers likely use this information to predict relationship outcomes in a less biased, more accurate way compared to people who are under the spell of romantic love. People in a relationship are capable of seeing undesirable traits in a partner and reaching pessimistic conclusions about the health of a relationship, but most people are not motivated to engage in this type of analysis.

In a meta-analysis of observers' ratings of personality across a wide range of settings, Brian Connelly from the University of Toronto and Deniz Ones from the University of Minnesota found that observers tend to agree with each other about others' personalities, and when multiple people rate one person, their average ratings are highly convergent with that person's self-ratings. What gave observer ratings of personality an edge in this meta-analysis was the fact that observer ratings of personality predicted future behavioral outcomes better than self-reports of personality. For example, when predicting two important life outcomes, academic achievement (e.g., grades in school) and job performance (e.g., rating by supervisors), friends' and family members' ratings of personality were much stronger predictors of these outcomes than self-reports.

A similar finding has emerged in studies comparing couples' ratings to observers' ratings to predict important relationship outcomes, such as long-term relationship satisfaction or divorce. Aggregating personality ratings from multiple observers provides more accurate and reliable estimates of personality, which in turn improves the predictive power of ratings from multiple observers when compared to individuals' self-reports. Presuming that your observers have your best interests in mind or, at the very least, are neutral in their opinion of your relationship, their vantage point outside the fog of infatuation affords them a clarity that is difficult for partners to achieve.

Here's the ideal scenario for garnering a range of personality ratings for a potential partner. Gather a group of friends with varying perspectives and viewpoints and have them go out with you and your partner. Although it may seem overwhelming to your partner to meet four or five of your friends at once, I like the idea of putting someone in a challenging but fair situation to see which traits emerge under pressure. These friends should receive no information or minimal information from you about your impressions of your partner or his or her personality. Everyone can be and probably should be perfectly pleasant toward your partner. After all, the report on your partner at the end might be favorable, and you don't want to scare your partner away with an aggressive interrogation session with your friends.

Afterward, gather informal ratings from your friends or, if possible, have them complete the personality scale included earlier and then average together all their ratings along with your ratings. Here's an example of a target, Blair, who is in the relationship, and her two friends rating her partner:

	Blair	Serena	Jenny	Total numbers of raters	Average
Openness	6	5	6	$\frac{17}{3}$	5.7
Extroversion	6	5	5	$\frac{16}{3}$	5.3
Agreeableness	4	5	4	$\frac{13}{3}$	4.1
Conscientiousness	3	2	1	$\frac{6}{3}$	2.0
Neuroticism	6	7	7	$\frac{20}{3}$	6.7

After calculating your partner's average scores, you can compare them to the Big Five scores in the table below to see if he or she is low, average or high for a particular trait compared to other people. Compared to the average person, Blair's partner is high on openness, average on extroversion, low on agreeableness, very low on conscientiousness and very high on neuroticism.

	Very Low	Low	Average	High	Very High
Openness	3.3	4.3	5.4	6.47	7.0
Conscientiousness	3.0	4.1	5.4	6.72	7.0
Extroversion	1.5	3.0	4.4	5.85	7.0
Agreeableness	3.0	4.1	5.2	6.31	7.0
Neuroticism	1.0	1.78	3.2	4.31	5.42

Now that you have a method to obtain relatively reliable assessments of the Big Five personality traits, the question is, which of those personality traits are most important when it comes to choosing partners who are most likely to create a love story that ends happily ever after?

THREE WISHES FOR PERSONALITY TRAITS

Among the thirty-five possible traits, which include the broad Big Five traits and the thirty sub-traits, which three provide the best predictive power for forecasting happily ever after? The Big Five profile of Blair's partner paints a picture of someone who is interested in seeking out novelty in a haphazard manner, but the uncertainty inherent in seeking out novel situations likely creates a high degree of anxiety and emotional instability, and if he or she does verbalize this emotional unrest to Blair, he or she does so in an unfriendly manner.

Although we might form a hypothesis about the ramifications of these Big Five traits over years in a relationship, it would be nice if researchers examined empirically what happens when people with different constellations of personality traits get into serious relationships. The ideal way to conduct studies of personality and relationships is to use reliable assessments of personality to assess personality *before* people meet their partners and then see if their scores predict: (1) how they form relationships, (2) how they act and feel in relationships and (3) whether their relationships are stable. Next, we'll see what researchers are finding about the most powerful personality predictors and why those traits allow you to see so clearly into a relationship future with potential partners.

Spotting Self-Saboteurs

Neuroticism is not easily perceived from online dating profiles or even from face-to-face meetings early in the dating process. Potential partners likely know just how costly displays of emotional instability are when trying to attract a mate, which makes it more likely that they will do their best to conceal this trait. However, outside observation by friends or family and careful attention to potential partners' histories and to their reactions under stress can be telling.

Neurotic individuals tend to have a history of turbulent and unstable relationships with others, including family and friends. They also tend to be prone to what looks like bad luck, but with time, one often sees that there are ways that their neuroticism evokes unfortunate events from their environment. For example, the negative emotional states that are characteristic of neuroticism cause people to make decisions that bring the most immediate reward but the worst long-term consequences. Consider those of us who wake up feeling like we don't want to go to work, a state that can occur in both neurotic and non-neurotic individuals. Neurotic individuals, being more prone to stronger negative emotions in that situation, might be more likely to choose the solution with the most immediate reward: stay in bed. Of course, this leads to a cascade of bad long-term consequences, such as getting in trouble at work, getting into an accident from being in a rush or just spilling coffee on themselves from being so disoriented.

One of the best ways to assess neuroticism in an individual is to pay extra close attention to what happens in stressful situations. Being highly reactive, neurotic individuals have difficulty modulating their reactions to intense situations, such as being caught in traffic or in a long security line at the airport, or having a disagreement with a coworker. The feeling is visceral when someone high in neuroticism is essentially "freaking out" about a stressful situation, and it's worthwhile to pay attention to your perceptions of potential partners in these situations. That's why getting outside observations and resisting the temptation to rationalize away negative behaviors from a partner's past are so important during the assessment process. I cannot stress enough how important it is to dispel any wishful thinking that neuroticism will simply go away because there are remarkably consistent findings about the tendency of neuroticism to remain constant across the life span.

Neuroticism is *the* most important personality predictor of future relationship satisfaction and stability. In one particularly well-conducted study by Richard Robbins and his colleagues, personality tests were administered to over seven hundred eighteen-year-olds and then the quality of, and the conflict and abuse in, their romantic relationships at ages twenty-one and twenty-six were tracked. What they found is that eighteen-year-old participants lower in emotional stability were significantly more likely than participants higher in emotional stability to be in relationships at age twenty-one and twenty-six that were lower in quality, higher in conflict and more frequently abusive. Low relationship quality at age twenty-one was associated with even more neuroticism at age twenty-six. In other words, being in a relationship did not "save" or "cure" people high in neuroticism.

Neuroticism is also predictive of lower relationship stability. In a follow-up study, Robbins and his colleagues found that neurotic participants were actually *more* likely to break up with partners who were low in neuroticism compared to partners who were high in neuroticism. It's as if neurotics could not stand their good fortune. Across numerous studies, neurotic partners are at a higher risk of relationship instability and divorce.

Catching the Cheaters

Partners low in impulse control and high in novelty seeking are a combination of high openness and low conscientiousness. To get a two-for-one deal on your wishes, let's just combine low to moderate conscientiousness and high levels of openness into a trait that personality psychologists call novelty seeking. The good news about partners high in novelty seeking is that they usually don't have the self-control to hide their personality for long. However, the confusing part about novelty seekers is that early in a relationship, they are fun, spontaneous and exciting. They also become easily and deeply absorbed in the relationship when they are first falling for you, and it feels great to have someone so invested and intrigued.

However, novelty seeking is associated with an increased risk for substance abuse, abusive behavior and explosiveness during discussions about conflict, which are all associated with less relationship satisfaction. Novelty seeking is also predictive of becoming bored more easily with doing the same thing, which is a recipe for disaster when it comes to sustaining a relationship with one person day after day. Novelty seekers' tendencies combine to make partners who provide less relationship stability. Novelty seekers are more likely to end a relationship because the "spark is gone." Essentially, they burn bright at the start, showing tremendous interest in you and the relationship, but are more likely to burn out in a rapid and spectacular fashion.

Importantly, novelty seekers are more likely to cheat, and there is probably no single behavior that poses more of a risk to relationship stability than infidelity. Roughly 30 to 40 percent of married partners will engage in infidelity at some point, and a single occurrence is often automatic grounds for considering terminating a relationship or marriage. What other relationship transgressions can ruin twenty years of marriage with one swift misdeed? The very description of the novelty seeker reads like a prelude to infidelity. Novelty seekers are:

1. More easily bored with the same thing (i.e., you).

2. More likely to seek out new situations or partners (i.e., not you).

3. More likely to put themselves in high-risk situations, such as going to a nightclub and drinking too much while looking at pretty lights and pretty women.

Nice Guys Are Better in Bed

Agreeableness gets a bad rap in the dating world, but it is one of the best predictors of long-term relationship happiness. People high in agreeableness tend to receive the dreaded "nice guy" or "sweet girl" label and do not seem like the types who would be the best candidates in pre-romantic times for clubbing someone over the head or vying for the alpha male position. Someone who is highly reactive (neurotic) and reckless (novelty seeking) would be the person I would draft to ward off threats in a highly dangerous mating environment. However, in modern lifelong partnerships, which last twice as long and often take place in tame suburban settings, there seems to be little value in choosing someone built for competitive survival.

In one meta-analysis of relationship satisfaction, Benjamin Karney at the University of Illinois and Tom Bradbury from UCLA found that the second strongest predictor of relationship satisfaction was sexual satisfaction. Here's the thing about sex and why satisfying sex is so important: there's one place to get it. One of my advisers in graduate school was fond of saying to new graduate students, "If your partner is bad at tennis, it's not a big deal, because you can go play tennis with someone else. If your partner is bad in bed, well, that's a big deal." Indeed, in monogamous relationships there is only one person who can provide this highly pleasurable and intimate behavior. Recall that in studies of the criteria for being in love, young adults in the United States identified two key components: lust and liking. There are few things more frustrating than lust not satiated.

Maintaining sexual satisfaction in a long-term relationship is best achieved when both partners are sexually satisfied, and emotional intimacy is a key facet of most female partners' sexual satisfaction. Someone who is genuinely agreeable is more empathic and more capable of intimacy. Men high in agreeableness are not only more likely to be kind, but are also more likely to keep the sexual desire alive in a relationship. Interestingly, when researchers have outside observers rate the physical attractiveness of couples, these ratings of physical attractiveness are not associated with the couples' reports of sexual satisfaction. Although there is probably some baseline level of attractiveness needed, this suggests that it is more the sexual skill of the partners and the quality of the relationship that predict long-term sexual satisfaction.

In a compelling study of agreeableness and relationship stability, Ted Huston and his colleagues from the University of Texas analyzed the data from a thirteen-year longitudinal study, which began when the researchers recruited 168 couples, who first participated in the study as newlyweds. Over the course of thirteen years, many variables were assessed including love, expressions of affection, responsiveness, negativity and contrariness. The researchers wanted to know which of these variables would distinguish the couples who ended up being happily married, being unhappily married, divorcing quickly and divorcing later over the course of thirteen years.

What they found was that one of the best variables for predicting who would stay married, even better than love, expressions of affection or negativity, was responsiveness, which is closely related to the personality trait of agreeableness. Couples who remained married were more responsive than those who divorced. However, the only variable that distinguished happily married couples from those who were unhappily married and from the two groups that divorced was contrariness, which is the variable most closely related to the personality trait of neuroticism.

PUTTING TOGETHER AN IDEAL PARTNER PERSONALITY

By utilizing all these findings on personality and relationship outcomes, it's possible to put together a more coherent picture of what a desirable partner personality would be. The partner would be high in neither neuroticism nor novelty seeking but would be high in agreeableness.

The good news is that you don't have to wish for partners who have spectacularly high levels of any particular personality trait, which means that unlike someone who wishes for a "hot-looking" partner or a partner with great wealth, you have a reasonable chance of finding someone who fits this prototype. If you choose someone who is very high in agreeableness, moderate in novelty seeking and moderate in neuroticism, let's say in the best seventieth percentile on agreeableness and fiftieth percentile on novelty seeking and neuroticism, then out of one hundred potential partners, you would have seven partners available.

Personality is a great category for diagnosing traits because it's specific enough to help you avoid the errors that occur when making complex "yes or no" relationship decisions, such as whether you will break up or stay together. The specificity and visibility of personality traits also allow you to combine your observations with the observations of friends and family to reach reliable assessments of potential partners' traits. You can then use these ratings of neuroticism, novelty seeking and agreeableness to predict with more accuracy who might provide a satisfying and stable relationship.

However, there can be instances when someone's personality is hard to assess. There might not be a strong consensus about a person's traits among you and your friends, or his or her personality might have a configuration that is difficult to understand. For example, what if someone is agreeable, emotionally stable, but very high in novelty seeking? Now you have to come up with a third wish, because you can't realistically expect that a wish for lower levels of novelty seeking in this promising partner will come true. There may be enough other positive signs in place for you to consider keeping in play this person who has just two of your three desired personality traits, and here's where it's helpful to look to other categories for additional wishes. In Chapter 8 and Chapter 9, I'll discuss others things you can wish for, so that you can select from a wider range of options when deciding upon your three wishes.

Next, we'll see how someone's positive dispositions can be enhanced or their negative dispositions diminished in homes where caregivers forge positive, loving relationships with their children. How partners psychologically attach to their caregivers during childhood is remarkably predictive of how they will attach to a romantic partner, and of whether their relationships will be satisfying and stable.

KNOWING WHEN YOU KNOW

When I was in elementary school, junior high and then high school, there were few places I enjoyed being more than in Ethan and Catherine's home. When I went to visit, we would do what you would expect at such an idyllic home as my godparents'. They would brew homemade cider, take me out to the cozy confines of the patio and sit me on the cushioned porch swing while they crafted riveting stories about a past that seemed more certain, gentler and happier. What we have been reminded of in this chapter is that nostalgia does not account for why couples like Grandpa Ethan and Grandma Catherine live happily ever after or create a home that is stable and warm. It's about two great individuals multiplying their great traits as a couple.

Ethan and Catherine fit the prototype described in this chapter to a tee: low neuroticism, moderate novelty seeking and high agreeableness. The environment they were able to create as a couple for the children they nurtured in their home, and for the random godchild who would wander by after school, was one that felt secure, understanding and loving. I suspect that there were rarely wild parties, fights to ascend to the top of the country club hierarchy or ridiculous trips to faraway lands.

While I am certainly not opposed to wild parties, VIP events with beautiful people or trips to faraway lands, those are not *essential* occurrences for building a love story that ends happily ever after. A life spent together in marriage is not always pure bliss and, in fact, inevitably entails a number of disagreements, stresses and responsibilities that will test partners to their limits. Under this kind of pressure, which will occur hundreds of times across many years, partners' true colors tend to flourish, for better or for worse. It depends on what type of partner you choose in the first place.

CHAPTER 8

Why the In-Laws Matter

Among the towering athletes on the sidelines, it was easy to miss the Big Man on Campus. Micah was the ten-year-old son of an assistant coach for the University of Maryland's men's lacrosse team, and the players affectionately called him the BMOC (Big Man on Campus). He was charged with helping the athletic trainers lug the medical equipment to the bench before games and with keeping some simple statistics during the games. Although the BMOC was not officially a member of the team, everyone treated him as if he belonged at the practices and games as much as anyone else, and he behaved with a precocious sense of teamwork that was deserving of that treatment.

A few years ago, Maryland was picked to contend for a national title. Micah and the rest of the team were particularly excited about an early season game against rival Princeton University. The Princeton game would surely be one of their toughest challenges of the season, and so a particularly strong feeling of anticipation pulsed through the huddle as the players gathered near the Maryland sideline. During those placid moments of pregame contemplation, no one could have imagined that the smallest person in that huddle would be the one to demonstrate the most strength in the hours to come.

Much like his father, Micah possessed a gentle demeanor, a tireless work ethic and an endless curiosity for the game. Micah's father was a great coach and an even better father, and our story is not one of romantic love, but rather about how compassionate love between a father and son, or a mentor and mentee, is what lays the foundation for how children will one day treat their romantic partners. Knowing how partners bonded with key caregivers during their childhood provides yet another window through which to see the future of your romantic relationships.

Micah had an unusually strong bond with Tyson, an all-American defender and one of the captains of this star-studded Maryland team. Tyson's brown Bieber-esque hair, handsome looks and athletic frame made him appear like a grown-up version of Micah. Having formed a brotherly bond that grounded both of them, Tyson and Micah sat together on plane rides and walked off the practice field together every day after playing catch. Micah's involvement with the team and his mentorship under Tyson imbued him with a sense of responsibility and action that was unusual for a boy his age.

The coach was fond of telling the players to simply "take care of your business" on and off the field, which essentially meant taking responsibility for doing what was right, when it had to be done. This mind-set of simply executing instead of overthinking had helped Micah, who was naturally shy, gain a sense of confidence and assertiveness, which he displayed not only with the team, but also in his friendships, schoolwork and participation in sports.

In the huddle right before the Princeton game, Tyson stood in the middle of the players, coaches and athletic trainers. He raised his fist, and with a tent of raised hands around him, Tyson calmed his teammates and focused their nervous energy as they looked to him for some final words of guidance. After reminding his teammates that they knew what needed to be done to win that day, he closed with a confident charge. "Let's take care of our business."

Toward the end of the second quarter, in the midst of a frantically paced game, Maryland was on the offensive, with Tyson quickly closing in on the goal. At the last moment, Tyson passed the ball to one of his teammates, before taking a vicious shot from a Princeton defender. Tyson's teammate launched the ball toward the goal, but it bounced off the top bar and quickly rebounded in the opposite direction. The red Maryland jerseys and the orange Princeton jerseys turned on a dime, and suddenly the space in front of the Princeton goal was vacated—except for Tyson.

He lay completely motionless on the far side of the field, and the medical staff burst onto the field to attend to him. When they slid to a stop alongside his crumpled body, the doctor and an athletic trainer quickly assessed whether he was still breathing and had a pulse. After a few quick seconds, the doctor estimated that his heart rate had plummeted to twenty beats per minute. The doctor took out his scissors to cut open Tyson's jersey and remove his pads, while the athletic trainer began the long sprint back toward the Maryland sideline to retrieve the AED machine, anticipating that they were going to have to shock Tyson's heart back to functioning.

Anyone will tell you that the difference between life and death can be a matter of seconds in these kinds of acute medical emergencies, and in the midst of her full sprint, the athletic trainer knew that every second counted. That's why everyone was so astounded that at the same time she began her sprint back to the bench, Micah burst through the players standing on the sideline and, with the AED in hand, ran at a full sprint toward the athletic trainer, moving his short legs as fast as they could go.

Micah met the athletic trainer at midfield, firmly passed her the AED and watched her sprint back to save the life of one of his best friends. The doctor grabbed the electrodes off the machine, set one beneath Tyson's right clavicle and the other alongside his left flank, and then they waited for what seemed like an eternity as the AED searched for any kind of heart rhythm from Tyson's unconscious body. In the meantime, Micah stood in the same spot where he had passed off the AED, and watched with fearful anticipation while his father grasped his shoulders, reassuring his son during this uncertain moment. When the AED diagnostics read "No Shock" and Tyson's heartbeats per minutes began quickly climbing into the fifties and sixties, the trainer and doctor looked at each other with relief that a crisis had been averted.

Seeing that the acute stages of the threat had passed, Micah fell to his knees and did what any ten-year-old boy would have been expected to do long before that moment: he cried.

WHY EVER AFTER WITH JUST ONE MATE?

It's remarkable that Micah was able to maintain his composure in the face of such a threat to the well-being of one of his closest interpersonal ties. What we will see in this chapter is that Micah's calm and courageous response was made possible by the secure attachments that had formed between Micah and his mother, Micah and his father, and even Micah and Tyson. Knowing the nature of individuals' attachments, whether they are secure or insecure, with caregivers during childhood allows us to make specific predictions about how their romantic relationships will function in adulthood.

Hundreds of studies conducted on attachment and relationship quality owe their foundations to a theory formed by psychologist

John Bowlby during the early 1950s. Bowlby had just graduated from Trinity College in Cambridge, where he studied psychology and pre-medicine, when he began working at an inpatient psychiatric center for delinquent youth. He observed that the youth often had a long history of disturbed relationships with their caregivers. What distinguished his thinking on that matter from most casual observations and half-baked academic theories was that he zeroed in on a way to elegantly describe the essential nature of the disturbed relationship with parents, which also provided testable hypotheses regarding how early experience affected later close relationship functioning.

Around the same time, research psychologist Harry Harlow was busy conducting studies with monkeys at his University of Wisconsin lab. Harlow was a controversial researcher, who some think pushed the ethics of animal research to their limits, but few debate the impact of his findings. He noticed that the baby monkeys were reluctant to let the research assistants remove the soiled cloths at the bottom of their cages. He wondered why the baby monkeys would show such an attachment to something that seemed disgusting. Harlow began conducting a series of studies that would challenge the strict behaviorist ideas that dominated in the 1950s. In particular, Harlow's studies would cast significant doubt on the strict behaviorist argument that babies showed attachments to their mother solely because mothers positively reinforced the babies' responses with breast-feeding.

To test whether baby monkeys showed a tendency to seek physical closeness to their mothers because of the food they obtained or merely because of the comfort they derived from being close to something that felt safe, he assessed which of two "surrogate mothers" baby monkeys preferred when their real mother was absent:

(1) a wire doll of a mother monkey with a bottle attached or (2) a soft cloth doll of a mother monkey with no bottle attached. If the mother-child relationship was based on behavioral principles of reinforcement, then the baby monkeys should choose the wire surrogate with food, but if they instead chose the cloth surrogate with no food, then this would suggest that something much different was driving mother-child bonds.

What he found was that baby monkeys regularly preferred the cloth surrogate with no food compared to the wire surrogate with food, which suggested that there was something about the "contact comfort" with the surrogates that motivated them more than even hunger. Harlow reasoned that if the regularity of physical contact and emotional intimacy were at the core of infants' experience, and at times were desired even more than food, then disturbances in this early close relationship might produce enduring disturbances in their ability to regulate their relationships with others. In a subsequent series of studies, which many would consider cruel by modern scientific standards, Harlow isolated baby monkeys from any kind of contact comfort during infancy and then observed great disturbances in their ability later to regulate their emotions, function cooperatively with peers and form mating relationships. These heart-wrenching disturbances in emotion and relational capacity remained pervasive and disabling throughout their life span.

Bowlby, Harlow and others have theorized and provided supporting evidence that animal and human infants are hardwired to seek secure bonds with their caregivers, because doing so increases their chances of survival. There are few species that are born as helpless as humans. Human infants are immobile, can't see much and are generally entirely inept without the help of caregivers. Similarly, adults without a strong tendency to remain close and attend to their offspring would be far less likely to see those offspring live to a reproductive age. Infants have only a few methods to fulfill their basic needs and their need for contact comfort and affection, and these include crying when they want to be held, fussing when they want to be fed and social smiling when they want to draw adults close.

If infants instinctively want to maintain closeness with and attentiveness from their caregivers for survival purposes, then caregiving that is erratic or remiss should cause infants distress at some fundamental level. Bowlby's inpatient delinquents who came from homes where they were neglected or randomly abused came to believe early on in childhood that their caregivers could not be relied upon, which planted seeds of anxiety and insecurity about the love and attentiveness of others who are close. In order to cope with this anxiety and insecurity, children create a set of beliefs and interpersonal behaviors that carry into adulthood and are disruptive to the quality and stability of their adult romantic relationships.

This groundbreaking research from the 1950s and 1960s laid the foundation for more nuanced ways of assessing whether human infants and adults become securely or insecurely attached and what their attachment style means for their adult romantic relationships. Researchers have shown not only that attachment impacts and predicts emotion, thought and behavior in the different forms of close relationships such as parent-child relationships, romantic relationships and platonic relationships, but also that there are predictable hormonal and neurological differences associated with secure versus insecure attachment styles.

So the in-laws do matter far beyond your enjoyment of family gatherings. Although your in-laws' approval or disapproval of your relationship can be facilitative or stressful for your relationship, they matter even more for your relationship, because the type of attachment they formed with their child, who is now your romantic partner, will be strongly predictive of how your partner treats you. Our desire to form reliable attachments with others, particularly with romantic partners in adulthood, is so strong that we are one of the few species that tries to form lifelong partnerships with one mate. Next, let's turn our attention to how you can use the tools researchers have developed to reliably assess a potential partner's attachment style and to how your partner's attachment style can help you see your romantic future.

UNCERTAINTY UNVEILS PARTNER'S ATTACHMENT STYLE

Before we get into what researchers know about attachment styles and romantic relationships, let's assess your attachment style and consider what your romantic partner's attachment style might be. I'll explain what your results mean a little later. There are many measures of adult attachment style. Some are questionnaires, and others are standardized interviews with psychologists. A relatively quick method originates from one of the first studies of adult attachment styles and romantic relationships, which was conducted by Cindy Hazan and Phil Shaver at the University of Denver. They presented study participants with one of three vignettes and asked which of those vignettes best described them as adults. I've included these vignettes below. Take a moment to consider which vignettes best apply to you and to a romantic partner:

Style One: I find it relatively easy to get close to others and am comfortable depending on them and having them depend on me. I don't often worry about being abandoned or about someone getting too close to me.

Style Two: I am somewhat uncomfortable being close to others; I find it difficult to trust them, difficult to allow myself to depend on them. I am nervous when anyone gets too close, and often, love partners want me to be more intimate than I feel comfortable being.

Style Three: I find that others are reluctant to get as close as I would like. I often worry that my partner doesn't really love me or won't want to stay with me. I want to merge completely with another person, and this desire sometimes scares people away.

The most reliable and most common method for assessing attachment in children is the "Strange Situation." Reviewing this method can tell us about how attachment functions across the life span. A star student of Bowlby's, Mary Main developed the Strange Situation method by beginning with the idea that if the attachment figure is meant to provide a sense of safety and nurturing for a child, then the absence of that caregiver should be upsetting, regardless of a child's attachment style. In the Strange Situation, a mother sits in the middle of a research room with the infant on her lap. When a light goes off on the wall behind the infant's head, the mother, following researchers' instructions, sets the child down and leaves the room without saying anything. As Main suspected and as just about any parent could tell you, the infant becomes distressed and begins to cry.

The interesting part of the Strange Situation occurs when the mother returns to the room after being gone for two minutes. She has been instructed to pick up the infant and to try to provide comfort. Infants tend to respond in one of three ways to this reunion with their caregiver:

1. **Secure** children stop crying relatively quickly. They take comfort from their mothers' physical presence and show appropriate amounts of affection. Secure children trust that their caregivers will be present and will attend to their needs, which allows them to respond to intimacy and love with a calm confidence.

If you could hear an imaginary inner monologue for secure children, it would go something like, "You left, but now you're here, so I guess everything is fine."

2. **Avoidant** children stop crying relatively quickly, as well, but they look aloof and dismissive. Avoidant children simply resolve not to care too much in the first place, which makes it easier not to be disappointed when their caregivers are unreliable or inattentive. The inner monologue for avoidant children when their mother returns would be, "Screw you for leaving. I don't need you, anyway."

3. **Anxious** children do not stop crying easily. They continue to be distressed and display clinging behaviors with their mother, and they alternate this desperate clinging with displays of anger toward their mother. Their inner monologue would be, "It's a disaster that you left me. Please don't go again, but I'm really mad you left."

Then something very interesting happens, which is the second behavior of interest during the Strange Situation. All around the room are toys, which have been placed at preselected distances from the mother. The toys are appealing to the children, and researchers are interested in measuring how far away from their mother the children will go to play with the toys. Remember that the Strange Situation starts with the mother leaving and the child being scared by her leaving, and so it is interesting that some of the children will now get off of their mother's lap and explore the space around them. After a couple of minutes hanging out with their mother after she returns to the room:

1. **Secure** children get off their mother's lap and begin to explore. They start with the toys that are closest to them, turning around every now and then to look at their mother, and sometimes picking up a toy to show her what they have found during their explorations.

2. **Avoidant** children also get off their mother's lap, but they do this more quickly than secure children. Avoidant children actually go the farthest and the fastest when exploring the toys around the room. However, they do not check back visually with their mother much or share their findings. They are on their own.

3. **Anxious** children take a long time to get off their mother's lap, and if they do, their exploration is limited and they look back at their mother in an almost paranoid fashion. They are narrowly concerned about their mother leaving again.

A fundamental proposition of attachment theory is that children need to know that they can rely upon their caregivers during times of distress. That's why the Strange Situation method is so clever. Having the mother leave the room at the start of the procedure places the child in a distressed state. Then, by observing what happens upon the mother's return, researchers can ascertain whether children have learned that they can rely upon their caregivers as consistent and loving figures who will protect and nurture them. Secure children have a mental model of their parents as being responsive to their needs. Avoidant children figure, "Why care?" because the caregiver cannot be relied upon. Anxious children cling and act out as a way to keep the parent from leaving again. After repeated instances of the child perceiving the degree to which his or her caregiver can or cannot be relied upon, these mental "models" of how caregiver-child relationships work become solidified as a template for close relationships in general.

What researchers have found repeatedly is that the way children react during the Strange Situation is predictive of how they will act in other contexts, such as in their relationships with their teachers, when separated from their mothers during the first day of school and when handling conflicts with their classmates on the playground. Secure children are at ease in their close relationships, avoidant kids don't form many close relationships and anxious kids cannot decide whether to cling or push others away.

You might be thinking that children's reactions to the Strange Situation sound a lot like the behavior of some of the adult romantic partners you've dated. Indeed, longitudinal studies provide strong evidence that there is a continuity between the attachment style individuals form in childhood and the attachment style they display in adulthood. You've probably guessed that the first vignette from the attachment measure is the secure attachment style, the second vignette the avoidant attachment style and the third the anxious attachment style. There is a striking similarity between the descriptions of attachment styles for children and those for adults, which is due to the strong continuity of attachment styles across the life span.

Glenn Roisman and his colleagues at the University of Illinois have conducted interesting research regarding the stability of attachment over time. Two fundamental questions with regard to attachment stability are whether children who are securely attached become securely attached adults and whether insecurely attached children become insecurely attached adults. What Roisman and his colleagues have found is that attachment shows some fluctuations over time, but overall, the attachment style people have as children is usually the attachment style they have as adults. Only 11 percent of eighteen-month-old children who were classified as anxious or avoidant in the Strange Situation were secure as nineteen-year-old adults.

Another study using the same sample found that, sadly, twenty-two of the fifty-seven children studied lost their secure attachment style by the time they were assessed as adolescents, because of maltreatment or trauma, whereas only six of the fifty-seven went from being insecure children to being secure adults. Although there can be changes in attachment styles from childhood to adulthood, insecure children become secure adults less often than secure children become insecure adults.

Perhaps the most relevant longitudinal studies for our review of adult attachment and romantic partner choice are a pair of studies conducted by Chris Fraley and his colleagues at the University of Illinois. They assessed 382 participants' attachment styles once a week for forty-five weeks to see how consistent their attachment styles remained across time. What they found was that the anxious attachment style and the avoidant attachment style were relatively consistent across weeks, which once again underscores that "what you see is what you get" when it comes to partner selection.

When securely attached adults are in the presence of someone they love, their heart rate declines and their respiration slows. In other words, the beloved's presence is calming, and it may make the other want to linger, to stay a little bit longer with this person whom they love. Even more notable is how securely attached adults react when the people they love are not in their physical presence. Securely attached adults are able to remain calm and content with just a mental representation of those they love because they trust that their loved ones will return and provide the same loving attention.

The idea that someone would react with dysfunctional panic to something as positive as love is mystifying. Anxiously or avoidantly attached adults may occasionally experience the same feeling of calm that accompanies love if they happen to let someone into their heart in the first place. However, the conundrum of close relationships for insecurely attached adults is that feelings of closeness and love trigger feelings of fear and the thought that the other might leave. So when researchers activate mental representations of loved ones (e.g., parents, romantic partners) in the laboratory, this elicits in anxiously or avoidantly attached adults a fear response, which can be measured in terms of their physical reactions. The mere thought of someone they love triggers increased heart rate, shortened respiration and tension in the muscles, as they experience the equivalent of the fight-or-flight response (cling to the loved one or flee the relationship). These physical reactions are simply a conditioned response between love and the reactions of close others: when you love someone, he or she leaves you. The almost instantaneous sequence of love and then fear triggers well-learned coping strategies.

The anxiously attached adult clings, becomes frightened by being so close and then pushes back in anger. Once the loved one begins, understandably, to distance him- or herself, the anxious adult clings once again, and so begins a long cycle of push and pull interactions. In the face of growing intimacy, the avoidantly attached adult simply leaves by closing down emotionally or simply removing him- or herself from the loved one's physical presence. This scenario sounds sad and confusing, and it is crushing and entirely bewildering for all involved.

Some may attribute avoidantly attached adults' stoicism in the face of distressing situations to an innate calmness or a high degree of maturity, but psychological researchers know that this is simply how avoidantly attached adults learned to cope with repeated exposure in childhood to inattentive caregiving and fearful, uncontrollable situations with their caregivers. The crude logic in the mind of a child who is not yet fully independent is something like, "If you don't get close to someone, then their leaving will not hurt as much." The intricate series of defenses that the avoidantly attached child and adult build over the years provides numerous triggers to alert them to impending intimacy, which activates reflexive reactions to keep others at a comfortable emotional distance and to stave off the seemingly unbearable fear of abandonment. These strategies work quite well if the goal is to stay emotionally protected. Researchers have found that avoidantly attached adults work more hours, advance further in their careers and are less likely to date seriously or to marry, which also means that they are less likely to suffer the heartbreak associated with unexpectedly losing someone they love.

A clever study by Chris Fraley and Phillip Shaver illustrates how avoidant attachment can manifest itself in adulthood. Researchers approached couples in the airport and asked them if they would complete some psychological measures, which included an attachment scale. They then thanked the couples and pretended that the study was finished. However, they then observed what happened once the couples boarded the plane. Like the Strange Situation did with children, this real-world observational study allowed the researchers to observe how the adults dealt with the threat of separation. When couples were not separating (the partners were boarding together), avoidant attachment scores were associated with more caregiving and less avoidance behavior. In other words, avoidantly attached people actually looked "not avoidant" when there was no threat of separation from their partner. However, when the couples were separating (only one partner was flying), avoidant attachment was associated with less physical contact, fewer caregiving behaviors and more avoidance behaviors. Thus, under circumstances of impending separation, avoidantly attached partners now looked perfectly avoidant. It's interesting that anxious attachment was not associated with any of the behavioral observation measures, such as contact seeking or sadness. The only significant result for anxiously attached partners was self-reports of distress, with those higher in anxiety reporting more internal distress.

ONE WISH FOR AN ATTACHMENT STYLE

It's probably clear by this point what you should wish for when it comes to attachment style. Although it may sound intuitive that choosing a securely attached partner would be the best bet, this common sense does not translate into people making the right wish in real life. To investigate whether people, regardless of their attachment style, prefer securely attached partners or a partner whose attachment style matches their own, Patricia Frazier and her colleagues at the University of Minnesota recruited 226 male and female college students who were not currently in dating relationships. Participants were told that they would look at nine "screening sheets" of potential romantic partners (think eHarmony profiles on paper) and that they might have a chance to go on a date with whomever they chose as most desirable from those screening sheets.

What Frazier and her colleagues found was that securely attached potential partners were not the most desired overall but rather that securely attached participants chose potential partners who seemed secure, anxiously attached participants chose anxiously attached partners and avoidantly attached participants chose avoidantly attached partners.

	Secure Partners	Anxious Partners	Avoidant Partners
Secure Participants	**52%**	39%	9%
Anxious Participants	36%	**53%**	11%
Avoidant Participants	28%	36%	**41%**

So it appears as though birds of a feather flock together when it comes to people preferring an attachment style that matches their own versus simply aiming for a securely attached partner. If you decide to use a wish on something other than choosing a securely attached partner, then it's interesting to see what you can expect in the long run from anxiously and avoidantly attached partners. Just how detrimental is insecure attachment, and what is your return on investment from secure attachment when it comes to reproductive fitness, relationship satisfaction and relationship stability?

Reproductive Fitness

Does attachment style predict physical health and the behaviors associated with successful mating? The existing evidence suggests that secure attachment may be a protective factor against disease and disease progression. In one study of over five thousand randomly sampled U.S. adults, Lachlan McWilliams and Jeffrey Bailey determined that attachment security, measured by the same measure you completed earlier in this chapter, was not related to an increased risk for twelve of thirteen different types of physical disorders. Conversely, anxious attachment was associated with an increased risk of experiencing headaches, chronic pain, stroke, heart attack, high blood pressure and ulcers. Avoidant attachment was associated with a 14 to 19 percent increased risk for pain disorders, such as headaches and chronic pain. Other studies suggest that once a disease, such as diabetes, has begun, insecure attachment is associated with poor management of the illness. There is little data regarding mating and attachment style, but avoidantly attached adults are less likely to marry or they marry later in life.

Relationship Satisfaction

In a meta-analysis of anxious and avoidant attachment and relationship quality, Tianyuan Li and Darius Chan at the Hong Kong Institute of Education aggregated the results of nearly eighty-eight different studies, which collectively included over sixteen thousand research participants. The prevalent hypothesis, which has generally been found across studies for the past two decades, is that insecure attachment should be associated with poor relationship quality. However, an important distinction is how avoidant attachment and anxious attachment relate to various relationship outcomes. Anxious attachment is characterized by more noticeable or active relationship emotions and behaviors, which is to say that when anxiously attached individuals are coping with their insecurity, their partners can see it or feel it. Avoidantly attached partners exhibit indifference and generally invest less in the relationship emotionally and show less affection, so their coping with insecurity is less obvious to the naked eye, but nonetheless, it would contribute to lower relationship quality over time compared to that of anxiously attached individuals.

What Li and Chan found was that anxiously attached partners reported less relationship satisfaction, fewer supportive behaviors and more negative emotions about the relationship. When observers rated the interactions of couples, it was determined that anxiously attached partners displayed more conflict behaviors and were engaged in more destructive interactions than less anxiously attached partners. Avoidantly attached partners reported less relationship satisfaction, lower feelings of connectedness, less supportive behaviors and higher levels of negative emotion in the relationship. As hypothesized, avoidant attachment was more strongly associated with relationship dissatisfaction, low feelings of connectedness and fewer supportive behaviors than anxious attachment. Conversely, anxious attachment was more strongly associated with conflicts during interactions than avoidant attachment.

Even though avoidant partners are "less obvious" about their attachment insecurity, the effects on relationship outcomes are substantial and widespread. There were few instances when anxious and avoidant attachment did not show a connection to detrimental relationship outcomes, such as destructive interactions, or to the absence of positive relationship processes, such as connectedness. Interestingly, one study suggested that elements of insecure attachment, such as a lack of comfort with closeness and anxiety about abandonment, affect marital quality because insecurely attached partners tend to be more neurotic, which in turn affects relationship quality.

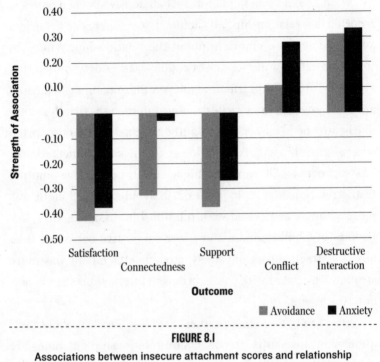

FIGURE 8.1
Associations between insecure attachment scores and relationship outcomes.

Relationship Stability

It's interesting to consider how an anxious or avoidant mind-set helps individuals to cope with caregivers who cannot be relied upon to provide support and love. Anxious children choose to cope with this potential unavailability of support and love by nervously keeping their caregivers close, and avoidant children choose to cope with it by keeping their caregivers at arm's length so as to not be disappointed. Given the continuity to adulthood of attachment styles, the goal of thinking, feeling and behaving in an anxious manner in an adult romantic relationship would be to keep the partner close, while for the avoidantly attached adult, the goal is the opposite, to keep the partner at a distance. So do anxiously attached adults achieve their goal of keeping romantic partners around, and do avoidantly attached adults maintain a close relationship with romantic partners when they don't want to get too close?

I found that there were surprisingly few studies of attachment and relationship instability, but two studies provide stark evidence of the differences between secure and avoidant attachment in terms of long-term marital outcomes. Eva Klohnen and Stephan Bera from the University of California, Berkeley, analyzed a thirty-one-year longitudinal study of women who were in the senior class at Mills College in 1958 and 1960. This impressive study has assessed participants' life course at twenty-seven, forty-three and fifty-two years of age. Klohnen and Bera found that women who were categorized as avoidant were significantly less likely than securely attached women to have ever been married by age forty-three. Even more striking was that only 24 percent of the securely attached women reported having a divorce in their lifetime, compared to 50 percent of avoidantly attached women.

In another study of attachment and lifetime marital history, researchers noted that participants who had been married multiple times were far less likely to be categorized as securely attached than a comparative college sample of unmarried young adults. There was a much lower proportion of secure attachment in the multiple marriages group (14 percent) compared to those in the never married group (47 percent). The multiple marriages group did not differ (38 percent) from the never married group (32 percent) in terms of anxious attachment, but those in the multiple marriages group (55 percent) were far more likely to be avoidantly attached than those in the never married group (15 percent).

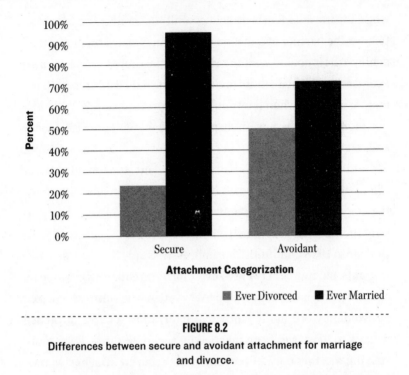

FIGURE 8.2
Differences between secure and avoidant attachment for marriage and divorce.

To be fair, I should mention that the unexpected paucity of data on attachment and relationship stability may owe partly to the fact that studies demonstrating a lack of an effect tend to be harder to publish than those in which effects are found. In this instance, if attachment styles are not predictive of breakups or divorce, then researchers or journal editors may be less likely to report the findings. One study that followed young couples for one year found that attachment did not predict who stayed together and who broke up. Although speculative, it may be that attachment predicts stability best when looking at long-term marital outcomes instead of short-term dating relationships.

Overall, your return on investment from steering clear of partners who are high in anxious or avoidant attachment, and seeking instead those who are high in secure attachment, is substantial. Partners who are high in secure attachment and low in anxious or avoidant attachment tend to have better health, to have partners who are more satisfied with the relationship and to experience more satisfaction with the relationship themselves. Choosing a partner who is not avoidant, but instead is secure, reduced divorce risk by half in one study.

NOT ALL HOPE IS LOST

When potential partners come from a dysfunctional home environment, where secure attachments with caregivers were an unlikely outcome from childhood, it does not mean that all is lost. Partners' difficult upbringing *never* excuses bad behavior toward you in a romantic relationship, because plenty of people are raised in less than optimal home environments and resolve to treat their partners well. This being said, a tough background should not instantly rule out potential partners, but it should alert you to take a closer look for possible attachment insecurity. After all, having unavailable or erratic caregivers was not their choice. Loving sounds so easy in theory, so why would people be fearful of someone they deeply love? If you have attachment insecurity, it takes time to develop insight about the relationship, to build your endurance for the struggle against yourself and to gather the courage to leap into building intimacy with someone, knowing that the closer you get, the more it will hurt if he or she leaves. This takes time because the beliefs that underlie an insecure attachment style were embedded long before you had the mental ability to make sense of the events and people driving them.

However, the studies of attachment suggest that some anxious or avoidant children, albeit a small proportion, do grow up to become "earned secures" (11 percent). You don't want to fall prey to positive illusions that someone who is severely anxious or avoidant in adulthood will change their attachment style anytime soon, but it's also the case that if potential partners are big enough to accept negative feedback about their patterns of relationship behaviors, mindfully adapt their behaviors based on that information and select situations or environments that are conducive to their best relationship outcomes, then you might pause to consider whether a relationship could end happily ever after.

One of the first goals for avoidantly attached adults trying to improve how they handle anxiety in their relationships is straightforward: not running. If they can manage to do this, then at least they have a chance of realizing that in times of relational uncertainty not everyone leaves. The goal for anxiously attached adults trying to improve their relationship outcomes entails something that may be a little more difficult initially: not panicking. I have begun to wonder whether the greatest tragedy is to lose your faith in the permanency of others and then to never let yourself experience something truly lovely. We'll see in the next chapter that a key to successfully taking the plunge for partners who are somewhat anxious, avoidant, neurotic or disagreeable is a willingness to moderate their relationship behaviors toward the loved one in a way that is healthy and sustainable.

THE SECURITY TO DO THE RIGHT THING

How should a child respond to the prospect of someone they love dearly leaving unexpectedly? As we've seen in this chapter, there are many ways that children experience the uncertain presence of their parents' love. Every year millions of parents emotionally or geographically abandon their children to pursue their own self-interests, such as career advancement, addictions or new lovers. For children, who have a limited cognitive ability to make sense of complex situations, the core problem is the same regardless of intent or circumstance. "How do I deal with the repeated threat that a loved one might physically or emotionally leave me?"

For the securely attached child and adult, there is little doubt about the ability and willingness of others to love them and attend to their needs, which frees them to devote their attention to other matters. Micah was observant of his father and loved his father deeply, but when they were on the practice field, doing their respective jobs, Micah did not need to be tethered to his father's side. He easily interacted with the trainers, coaches and players because he could trust that his father would protect him and attend to him in a time of need or even if Micah were to get out of line.

I'm not sure that an anxiously attached or avoidantly attached child could have handled the situation on the lacrosse field the way Micah did that day, because such a child would have been so physiologically aroused and psychologically distressed by seeing a loved one potentially "leaving." Through no fault of their own, but rather owing to reactions that helped them cope with incomplete bonds with their caregivers, the anxious child would have melted down and the avoidant child would have shut down.

In the face of a threat, Micah braced himself with the self-confidence that comes with secure attachment, and this gave him the courage to act and find the AED as quickly as possible. In this way, he was able to attend to his friend better than anyone else on that sideline and his way of viewing relationships would one day make him a wonderful husband and father.

When the head coach asked Micah at the end of the game how he had found the resolve to retrieve the AED, Micah simply replied, "I was just taking care of my business. . . ."

CHAPTER 9

Red Flags in Relationships

When I worked at therapy clinics as a doctoral student, I learned that you could often glean quite a bit of information based on what you saw from your clients in the waiting room. One memorable waiting room moment happened during the spring of 2001 at the student health center at the University of Minnesota. I had been working with a perfectly likable couple, Will and Katie, whose newlywed first year had been a tumultuous one. As I went to pick them up in the waiting room before our fourth session of couples therapy, I knew from the first moment I laid eyes on them that this would easily be the wildest session yet.

Will was a graduate student in environmental science, and his rugged facial features, husky 225-pound frame and array of fleece vests made him appear like a young man straight out of an Eddie Bauer catalog. He sat at attention, his hands set firmly on his corduroy-covered knees, his large frame tilted forward onto his toes, his gray eyes wild with alertness. I could have sworn that he was sweating in the chill of the waiting room, but it was difficult to tell with the large piece of gauze that was taped to the middle of his forehead. His wife, Katie, taught Tae Bo and spinning classes at a hard-core gym downtown. She looked so taut, badass and intense all at once, which led to me being shocked when I found out that her smile was remarkably warm and her voice was as soothing as a PBS voice-over.

She sat to the left of Will, looking nervously in the direction of his darting gray eyes, monitoring his facial expression for some sign of grace. You didn't need to be a psychologist to know that Will had had his head hurt and that Katie probably was the one to inflict that hurt. What became the most interesting was trying to figure out what series of thoughts, emotions and behaviors led up to this dramatic moment. Before they sat in the waiting room, on pins and needles, before Katie took Will to get the bandages, and before she threw the beer bottle at his head the previous night.

On that fateful night Katie had come home from a long day at work, which included teaching classes from 6:30 a.m., and the last thing she wanted to do was have to clean the house. Will had spent the day at home, working on his dissertation, which was now six months overdue. He had left once during the day to go to the doughnut shop for a treat of some doughnuts, and upon returning home, he had left a trail of shoes and dirty socks on his way to the television for his afternoon session of *Gilligan's Island* reruns.

A self-admitted clean freak, Katie saw the trail of sloth, and on this night it was more than she could bear. She began yelling at Will before he could even see her from his slouched position on the couch, and by the time he sat up and turned around, she was in his face. Her icy blue eyes were filled with rage, and she was on a rant about his nasty socks on the floor, his laziness, his lack of appreciation for her hard work, and she punctuated her case against him by asking, "What do you have to say for yourself?" That was when Will made another very poor choice. He replied, "Take it easy, Katie. They're just socks. . . ."

At this point, Katie pushed him off the couch with a powerful Tae Bo shove and walked toward the kitchen island in disgust. Will did an awkward roll and stumbled to his feet while making his last unhelpful comment of the night. "Bitch!" That was when Katie picked up Will's half-empty microbrew beer bottle by the neck, spun around like a baseball pitcher unraveling from a windup and hurled the bottle like an axe. Her accuracy was remarkable. Then an ambulance came, followed by the police, and now they sat in my office, wondering where they had gone so wrong.

IS THIS RELATIONSHIP CRAZY, OR AM I CRAZY?

It's unusual for violent explosions to come completely out of the blue. There are often aspects of the relationship that predict the risk for angry feelings toward a partner or aggressive behaviors. We've found in our studies of breakups that when people look back on their relationships, they can't believe that they didn't pay more attention to red flags from brief, but telling interactions. For example, there are those moments when you catch a partner looking just a little too adoringly for a little too long at someone he or she says is "just a friend," and you know that it's indicative of potential trouble. A friend told me after breaking up with a verbally abusive man that she should have known something was wrong when a flight attendant nicely asked him to sit down and she heard him mutter under his breath, "I'm never fucking wrong. . . ."

In hindsight, these flashbulb moments seem so vivid and diagnostic of what was to come, but at the time, they are easily brushed away as insignificant blips on the relationship monitor. On the other hand, you don't want to overreact about your partner's friends, because then you're that "jealous partner." Similarly, sometimes things said in frustration really are just benign comments that don't mean anything in the long run.

The question is how to know which events in relationships are clear markers of relationship dysfunction. The task is to distinguish which traits in partners are annoying but inconsequential in the long run and which traits are red flags for serious problems in the future. It's important to keep in mind that we're not very good at making decisions about complex problems that are framed as "yes or no" questions. So we need some specific and observable ways to think about the interactions that matter in the early stages of relationships, among thousands of possible interactions.

Fortunately, researchers have identified clear markers of dysfunction in ongoing relationships that give us a window into how long-term dissatisfaction and instability emerge. What we'll see in this chapter is that if you remain uncertain about your wishes even after examining a partner's personality and attachment style, you can look to red flags, which might provide the last thread of evidence you need to make clear decisions. We'll see that paying attention to a partner's thoughts about why problems occur in relationships, their patterns of actually discussing problems and their responses to positive events can help us forecast future relationship satisfaction and stability.

Everyone in a close relationship makes mistakes during the course of a day or a week, but it's not one instance of a negative or positive behavior, but rather the ratio of positives to negatives, that matters in the long run. John Gottman calls this cumulative ratio of positive to negative behaviors an "emotional bank account." The idea is that each partner can deposit in the couples' account emotional capital (e.g., satisfaction) with positive behaviors and withdraw emotional capital from the couples' account with negative behaviors. However, the goal for any couple is to have a satisfying relationship, not just a relationship that is barely good enough. Thus the ratio maintained needs to have more positives than negatives. In other words, couples need to maintain a positive balance in their emotional bank account, but just how much of a balance do they need to maintain?

A study by John Gottman and Robert Levenson illustrates how the ratio of positives to negatives predicts long-term relationship satisfaction and stability. Seventy-nine couples were recruited to come into the lab and discuss pressing problems in their relationships. The problem-solving discussions were coded for positive and negative behaviors. Four years later, the researchers followed up with the couples to assess their marital satisfaction and to learn whether they had separated or divorced.

What they found was that couples who were satisfied and stable, compared to those who were dissatisfied or divorced, maintained a ratio of five positive behaviors to every one negative behavior. Consider the following example to see just how difficult this ratio can be to maintain. Katie comes home to see that Will has picked daisies from the garden for her, left her a sweet note and made the bed. Later, Will gives her a big hug and tells her that she looks nice. These five positive behaviors, and thus the positive balance in the emotional bank account, could be wiped out by his single act of careless behavior when he says, "I wish you looked nice more often."

During the early stages of dating, it's important to keep an eye open for which concerning behaviors translate into big withdrawals from the emotional bank account and present a growing risk as the relationship moves forward. An overly optimistic view of the risks and potential benefits of investing in a particular partner is the same kind of blind optimism that nearly bankrupted big banks around the world a few years ago. So that you avoid a similar crisis with the emotional bank account of your relationship, the sections to come will show you what researchers have found about key markers of thoughts about problems, problem-solving behaviors and responses to positive behaviors. These key markers can help you determine which partners are risky investments *before* you invest. Being on the alert for key relationship markers can mean the difference between a relationship staying afloat or going bankrupt.

THINKING ABOUT WHY

One thing that distinguishes humans' intellectual capabilities from those of other animals is their ability to think about why. Humans can ponder topics as broad as "Why do I exist" and as mundane as "Why do boys' bikes have bars across the top but girls' bikes do not?" Sometimes the answers to these questions can seem unknowable, and at other times, the reasons we're provided are unsatisfactory or incomplete, such as, "because if a girl hit the bar, it could hurt."

These tendencies to look for causes or explanations as to why events occur is what psychologists call "attributions." We are wired to automatically search for causes of relationship events; part of what makes us human is asking why things occur. In relationships, we are particularly motivated to figure out why our partners do certain things, because knowing why they did something helps us predict whether they will be likely to help us or harm us in the future.

Of course, attributions' usefulness hinges on accurately identifying the real cause of a problem or a desirable outcome. For example, if your computer monitor goes blank, you can try a number of things—you can push buttons to get the right setting, take the monitor apart to look for an internal problem, call customer service to get outside help or hit it in an act of desperation—but the monitor won't turn on if the real problem is that the plug fell out of the socket. Similarly, barking up the wrong attribution tree in romantic relationships can cause all kinds of frustration and distress for you and your partner, while doing nothing to help you identify what is actually causing a relationship problem and how you might best fix that problem.

We can go back to a framework in Chapter 1 to examine attributions in ongoing relationships. Recall that there is the self (you), your partner, your interaction (relationship) and circumstances surrounding the relationship (environment). Each of these broad categories could cause good things or problems in a relationship, but knowing how to decipher attributions in an accurate and balanced manner is easier said than done.

Imagine that you are late for dinner and your partner must sit alone at a restaurant and wait for twenty minutes until you arrive. There are four possible attributions he or she could make to account for your tardiness, including:

1. I'm worthless. She's (He's) leaving me. (Self)

2. She's (He's) irresponsible. (Partner)

3. We didn't communicate clearly. (Relationship)

4. There must be unexpected roadwork on the highway. (Environment)

It's difficult to tell which of these attributions is accurate without knowing the couple's specific situation, but it does seem clear that some of the possible attributions are better bets than others. If there are spontaneous road closures on the highway you are taking to the restaurant, then the environmental attribution seems like the most accurate and the most useful one. This external cause for your lateness would also elicit a relatively benign emotional reaction from your partner.

The first problem with leaping to partner attributions is that they can be inaccurate. Even if the tardy partner is generally irresponsible, in this instance it's the environment, not the partner, that is causing the tardiness. The worst kinds of negative partner attributions fall into three groups, and they have varying degrees of toxicity:

1. **Stable** attributions are those liabilities that are consistent over time and are unlikely to change.

2. **Global** attributions are undesirable traits that affect many parts of an individual's life or relationship.

3. **Intent** that is associated with attributions is the icing on the cake. The assigning of intent means that the individual is being blamed for intentionally causing a problem.

The second problem with partner attributions is that they tend to incite strong negative emotional reactions in the self. In the restaurant scenario your waiting partner fumes and builds up resentment with each passing minute. The third problem with partner attributions is that if the "wronged" partner decides to share insights about the attributions for the problematic situation, then the chances of that discussion going well are near zero. For example, imagine if he or she says something along the lines of, "I know what's wrong. It's the fact that you're always so irresponsible." If you find yourself in a relationship in which you are consistently blamed for disagreements or for things going wrong, then you are right to interpret this as a huge red flag going forward with this partner.

I should mention that there is the possibility in some cases that partner attributions are not exaggerations at all, but are accurate. If that's the case and you're the one voicing the partner attributions, then there's probably no reason to keep dating that person. The future doesn't look bright if there are so many trait-like flaws in your partner. On the other hand, if someone is piling trait-like attributions on you, constantly berating you about who you are fundamentally, then you might question their lack of sensitivity.

It's one thing for your partner to point out specific negative behaviors and events for which you are accountable if, after considering a broad range of causes, including his or her own culpability (self), your partner believes that his or her assessment is accurate. These types of conversations are promising, because they address specific instances and specific behaviors that you can improve or work on in the relationship. However, a conversation in which someone tells you in a thoughtless manner that you're irresponsible, incompetent or unworthy is rarely going to turn out well.

Your return on investment for avoiding partners who make a large number of partner attributions is high for future satisfaction and stability. In one particularly telling study, Benjamin Karney from the University of Illinois and Thomas Bradbury from UCLA analyzed data from a four-year longitudinal study of newlywed marriage. Couples' attributions, marital satisfaction and divorce were assessed every six months over the course of the four-year study. What they found was that trait-like partner attributions for negative events in the marriage strongly predicted declines in marital satisfaction. Furthermore, couples making more partner attributions were more likely than couples making fewer partner attributions to divorce. Across numerous other studies, trait-like partner attributions are associated with less relationship satisfaction, more unhelpful conflict behavior and a higher risk of instability.

DEMANDING AND WITHDRAWING

If a partner has a thought about your relationship, it's not guaranteed that you will ever know about it. Sometimes a partner has negative thoughts or legitimate concerns about you or the relationship and never does anything to explicitly let you know about it. Being open and honest about concerns or significant problems is generally a good idea for the health of a relationship, because otherwise these seeds of discontent tend to fester and grow into bigger problems. So conflict is not inherently bad in a relationship, and it's usually inevitable. However, the ways in which a couple handles those conflicts is a telling marker of future relationship satisfaction and relationship stability.

One of the hallmark behaviors of dysfunctional relationships is what researchers call a demand/withdraw pattern. The partner who demands is not really asking kindly for something, but rather conveys his or her request with a small to large degree of blame, pressure to change, nagging or complaining. The partner who withdraws simply gives up on trying to discuss the problem and may even actively avoid any discussion about a problem when the other partner broaches the subject.

Demands that are made with just a tinge of pressure or blame at first may escalate over time as partners become immune to the small doses of negativity packaged with the demands. Eventually, the partner making the demands *begins* the discussion with intense displays of blame, pressure and aggression, a conflict resolution strategy that looks like the wartime philosophy of hitting the enemy with initial shock and awe. The withdrawing partner just needs to shut down more, but even the best withdrawing partners have their limits in the face of persistent and intense demands.

The occasional "giving in" to the demands of the partner by the withdrawing partner reinforces the dysfunctional pattern. The demanding partner gets what he or she wants (e.g., socks are picked up). The withdrawing partner gets a respite from the nagging or pressuring (e.g., no more beer bottles are hurtled). This creates the same sort of reinforcement that casinos use to hook people on gambling at slot machines, which is reinforcement that occurs at unexpected times. People don't know whether they will win after one pull or twenty pulls of a slot machine, and this motivates them to keep spending money. In other words, winning is a little bit sweeter when there's an element of surprise. Similarly, a withdrawing partner's compliance tends to come at random intervals, which makes it more likely that the other partner will continue to make demands.

No one is more to blame in this scenario, because demanding partners can do a better job of making calm, clear requests, whereas withdrawing partners can do a better job of showing some engagement in important issues. Unfortunately, the more one partner withdraws, the more the other intensifies the demands, which leads to more pronounced withdrawal, and this downward spiral picks up so much speed that it sweeps away any hopes of either partner getting his or her needs met.

If you find yourself with a partner who exemplifies this kind of demanding style—the kind tinged with partner blame, pressure and aggressive undertones—and these demands occur across many of the requests in or discussions about the relationship, then you might want to consider wishing for a partner who does not have this sort of interaction style. Similarly, if you are with a partner who withdraws from any sort of reasonable request or serious discussion about the relationship, then you might want to wish for someone without this retreating style, because trying to play alone at a relationship is no fun at all.

The costs of the demand/withdraw pattern are substantial for long-term relationship satisfaction and stability. Christopher Heavey and his colleagues from UCLA brought forty-eight couples into the lab to investigate the associations between demand/withdraw patterns of interaction and long-term relationship satisfaction. Women and men each chose a problem to discuss for ten minutes, and their interactions were video recorded for research assistants to code later for demand/withdraw patterns. Two and half years after this interaction in the lab, couples were contacted again and their relationship satisfaction was assessed. What the researchers found was that high levels of male and female demanding, regardless of whether the partners were discussing the male or female partner's issues, showed a large association with both partners being less satisfied at time one and time two. They also found that when couples were discussing the problem of the woman's choosing, higher levels of female demanding and male withdrawal observed in the lab at time one were associated with significant drops in satisfaction over the course of two and a half years.

In a study of demand/withdraw patterns and relationship stability, John Gottman and Robert Levenson recruited seventy-eight married couples, who were observed in a lab while discussing a conflict and then were contacted four years later for assessments of their relationship satisfaction and stability. What they found was wife-demand/husband-withdraw patterns observed in the lab were associated with a significant increase in divorce risk four years later. Anecdotally, I have seen the effects of chronic demand/withdraw patterns on dozens of couples like Will and Katie in couples therapy. My feeling when sitting in a room with a couple, having heard them describe years of increasing frustration over demands unmet and shrinking withdrawal from the marriage in general, is that this phenomenon takes a toll insidiously on once vibrant and loving couples, leaving them exhausted and demoralized.

CAPITALIZING ON THE GOOD STUFF

I always find myself a bit vicariously exhausted after reviewing the negative outcomes associated with partner attributions and demand/withdraw patterns, so let's investigate something more positive, but equally as powerful, for predicting relationship quality. Psychological researchers have overwhelmingly focused on studying negative aspects of relationships, such as irrational beliefs, poor conflict management and divorce, but the empirical reality is that when most couples first marry, there is far more good than bad. While it makes good sense to think about how to prevent negatives from ruining the five-to-one ratio of positive to negative behaviors, it also seems foolish not to think about how to increase the positives.

Shelley Gable at the University of California, Santa Barbara, has shown through a rigorous program of research how couples can amplify the many positive moments in relationships. Almost every day there are positive events that happen in the life of each partner. Those positives can range from small things, like finding a lucky penny or receiving a thank-you from a coworker, to bigger things, like getting a bonus at work or receiving a huge promotion. The beauty of positive events is that regardless of their magnitude, when you share them, you afford your partner a great window of opportunity to build intimacy with you and to grow the relationship in general.

Capitalization is when you share a positive event and your partner matches your degree of enthusiasm in his or her response. Studies have shown that people share daily positive events, both small and large, with their partners about 70 percent of the time. There is a natural motivation for someone to witness or share in your accomplishments or simply your moments of good fortune, and the act of sharing good news helps to validate your personal experiences. However, personal behaviors in relationships never take place in a vacuum, and so your partner's *actual* response and your *perception* of your partner's response are key to successful capitalization.

Professor Gable provides a straightforward way to understand actual responses and perceived responses to sharing positive news. Partners can respond actively or passively and in constructive or destructive ways to positive news, which produces four possible responses. The best of those four responses is clearly the active/constructive one. Like with many things in relationships, there are more ways to get it wrong than to get it right, but if you do get it right, the benefits are substantial.

	Constructive	Destructive
Active	Partner is enthusiastic and engaged about the positive news.	Partner says something critical about the positive news.
Passive	Partner has a positive attitude but says little and shows little outward enthusiasm.	Partner discounts the sharing by changing the subject or ignoring the remark.

Collectively, these data suggest that couples have a great opportunity to amplify the positive feelings in a relationship on a daily basis. Since couples share positive events with each other 70 percent of the time, there are opportunities almost each day for capitalization. Furthermore, the person sharing the news is already in a good mood about the event, and so all the other partner has to do is respond in a way that is enthusiastic and interested. What numerous studies have shown is that couples who consistently experience capitalization from the positives they share with each other reap a number of rewards both at the personal and relationship level.

In one exemplary study, Professor Gable and her colleagues assessed capitalization, relationship satisfaction, conflicts and intimacy in eighty-nine married couples every day for two weeks. Controlling for couples' initial levels of marital satisfaction, they discovered that capitalization that was active-constructive was associated with more daily marital satisfaction and stronger feelings of intimacy. Conversely, missed capitalization attempts by male partners were associated with their female partners being less satisfied, reporting more daily conflict and experiencing weaker feelings of intimacy.

What do the results from studies of capitalization tell us about wishing for traits in a partner? I see three essential things to look for when assessing whether a partner will help grow your relationship with positives:

1. Choose a partner who is willing to share positive events. Although most people share their small and big positive events frequently, not everyone does, and those with traits such as avoidant attachment may feel too fearful to risk a partner not being responsive to their positive news.

2. Choose a partner who is attentive and empathic enough to know just how much a positive event means to you in the larger scheme of your life. This kind of partner responds with genuine enthusiasm to your good news because he or she is invested in your success and well-being.

3. Choose a partner who has enough self-esteem to believe that your enthusiasm about his or her positive news is genuine. Partners with low self-esteem may be prone to actively or passively discounting your validation of their good news or your feelings of genuine happiness about their accomplishment.

GROWING YOUR RETURN FROM RELATIONAL WISHES

Overall, investing in partners who grow your emotional bank account increases your returns exponentially over time. By avoiding potential partners who are prone to making partner attributions and to demanding or withdrawing during important discussions, and by seeking those who are likely to enhance the positives in your relationship through capitalization, you will have a powerful base for finding a happy and enduring relationship. You would reap rewards on a daily basis from choosing a partner based on the relational markers reviewed in this chapter, just as you would from investing in a partner who is emotionally stable or securely attached.

Negative events and problems are experienced by even the happiest couples on a regular basis, so having a partner who does not jump to partner attributions that attack your character, or who is willing to take a look at his or her contribution to relationship problems, gives you a small but important return every time an issue arises. Likewise, having a partner who makes reasonable requests or who is engaged in important discussions about the relationship gives you an advantage every time there is a discussion about important relationship issues. Finally, there are almost daily opportunities to grow the natural returns from sharing positive events, and so having a partner who is attentive and enthusiastic about celebrating your successes will make life a whole lot more enjoyable over time.

It's not that any single one of these factors is a deal breaker in a relationship, and hopefully, you won't often have to use a wish on avoiding tendencies to make partner attributions, to engage in demand/withdraw patterns or to fail at capitalization. However, you want to be attentive to markers that can drain an emotional bank account and to opportunities to grab a partner who is skilled at growing positives.

NO MORE BITTER BEER FACE

When they first came into couples therapy, Katie and Will both identified the presenting problem on their pre-appointment paperwork, writing, "We are worried that our relationship is so bad that we might get a divorce." Although this statement was somewhat informative, it didn't really provide much traction for thinking specifically about what might be going wrong and about what the prognosis might be for the future of their relationship. That's where research proves useful. It has given us clear markers of how relationships often sour and disintegrate across time, and with these we can more quickly and efficiently make sense of *why* and *how* relationships get so bad.

Katie and Will recounted being so attracted to each other and in love with each other during those first few months after they met four years earlier. It was in one of Katie's Tae Bo classes at the University of Wisconsin–Madison where she became so drawn to Will's average facial features, powerful build and emotional stability. From the back of the room, Will had admired Katie's pronounced facial features, fit body and intensely competitive spirit. They thought it was a case of opposites attracting, and there were so many likable things about Will and Katie as individuals.

There was something about being in a relationship, about the simmering of their traits together, that brought out the worst in both of them. Will's already trait-like levels of low self-esteem were made worse by Katie's tendency to jump to partner attributions about Will being "lazy" and "weak." Katie found Will's lack of responsiveness to even the most reasonable requests for basic relationship maintenance infuriating, and it produced in her an intense form of demanding, which Katie thought was behind her after months of individual therapy in her teens.

I don't know what happened to Katie and Will, because they eventually dropped out of couples therapy unexpectedly. Who knows if it was Will, Katie or both of them who decided that they should not come back to continue working on their relationship? The unexpected dropout rate in psychotherapy is 40 percent on average, and so you don't take it too personally when couples don't return. Maybe it was because I made mistakes or maybe they didn't like me or maybe I was not doing things they found helpful—I'm open to all those possible explanations. Psychotherapy researchers have speculated that couples begin to see clearly the deeper problems in a relationship when therapy is progressing well. This might well have been the case for Katie and Will and might explain why they did not return to therapy.

Katie and Will's story is interesting because it illustrates that unhappy relationships are a complicated mixture of thoughts, behaviors and missed opportunities, which can be very difficult to deconstruct. We began to figure out that Will did, in fact, sit around most of the day playing video games on the computer instead of working on his dissertation. Will was objectively sloppy and was not helpful with housework, and I saw with my own eyes in therapy just how dismissive he could be of Katie's requests. Katie's obsessions about cleanliness turned out to be at diagnosable levels of obsessive-compulsive disorder. She worked seventy hours every week between the gym and another job doing filing at a medical office, which still left them financially stressed much of the time because Will no longer had income from being a teaching assistant. He had declined funding to have more time to work on his dissertation.

All these things were seemingly "true" or "accurate." It's this idea of accuracy that can often be lost in research about relationship dysfunction. Researchers and therapists can get so caught up in the idea that partner attributions and demand/withdraw patterns are associated with less satisfaction and stability. The therapeutic inclination can be to eradicate partner attributions and have people start blaming something else, such as themselves or environmental factors, and to stop demanding or withdrawing.

However, partners are neither perfect as individuals nor perfectly matched, even in the best scenarios. All partners have some traits that are less desirable, and those traits can drive us crazy. When those traits go unmitigated and manifest themselves as chronic meanness, cruelty or a lack of concern, then people are right to point out these concerning characteristics and to ask for some mindful changes on the part of the guilty party. When we are guilty of allowing our worst traits to get the best of us and of allowing those traits to consistently have a negative impact our relationship, reasonable requests for discussion should not be ignored or dismissed. No partner is perfect, and part of a relationship is showing a consistent effort to manage your own weaknesses, while showing some consistent grace when it comes to your partner's weaknesses.

To show meaningful effort and to know where to allocate their grace, couples have to first face the depth and breadth of what really drives problems in their relationships. This can be daunting for any couple, and I sometimes wondered if I pushed Katie and Will too fast toward this moment of truth. It's part of the second-guessing that comes with being a psychologist: even when you follow treatment protocols known to be effective from clinical trials, knowing how to help couples eliminate unhelpful coping strategies and grab on to hard truths is sometimes an imperfect art.

Eventually, Katie and Will began to gain insight into the glaring problems that were the real sources of their dissatisfaction, and this process exposed oversimplified partner attributions and hasty demand/withdraw patterns as mere shadows of their core problems. What lay at the core of their difficulties was personal liabilities that were in place before they ever met in class, kissed for the first time or exchanged vows to "have and to hold until death do you part." Katie's partner attributions regarding Will's laziness and avoidance were accurate, and her demands for change were an overly intense way to communicate her hopes that he would actively manage those liabilities. Will's automatic intuition that almost any request from Katie was an unreasonable result of her obsessions or aggressiveness led to a reflexive withdrawal from interactions, which sabotaged any hope of successful resolutions.

Will and Katie could have better managed their attributions and problem-solving discussions, but one wonders whether they would have signed up for a lifelong contract had they fully considered the traits of the self and the partner, and how those would interact in a relationship, *before* they said, "I do." The task you have when you're single is to be honest with yourself about whether your partner's traits give you a good chance of success as a couple. In the past couple of chapters, you've learned how to identify key traits, such as personality traits, attachment styles and relationship patterns, based on the best psychological science available. This arms you with powerful tools to identify hard truths about partners before it's too late and to see hopeful truths about partners who give you the best chance of finding enduring love.

CHAPTER 10

How to Make Your Wishes Come True

Daniel stood at the back of the luxurious Brooklyn penthouse, by a wall of large bay windows overlooking the East River, and dispassionately watched the hundreds of beautiful guests clinking their champagne glasses as 2012 was now only minutes away. He watched the beautiful people clad in party clothes nervously scan the room for someone to kiss before midnight struck. His eyes eventually rested on his girlfriend, Sophia, who stood in the middle of the party, getting ready to kiss someone who was not Daniel. As he watched his love life slipping from his grasp, he let his head fall backward against the cold glass.

Daniel and Sophia had met one year earlier in an exclusive Las Vegas nightclub. Among the shiny socialites, Sophia had stood out as one of the most stunning, and so Daniel was shocked when she approached him, because his Midwest look was "adorable." A spotlight seemed to follow Sophia wherever she went, and when they walked into that Brooklyn penthouse for that fateful New Year's Eve party, she looked particularly striking. She perched above almost everyone else in her five-inch heels, she was mysteriously tan for someone living in Manhattan in the middle of the winter and her facial features were sharp enough to cut glass. She glided about the room, effortlessly inserting herself into ongoing conversations with strangers and flashing a winning smile with a flirtatious twinkle in her eyes. That flirtatious twinkle had captured the attention of one of the guests, a former football player with the Giants or the Jets, or some team of which Daniel was not a member. That was why it didn't surprise Daniel when he saw Sophia caressing the tight end's pectorals through the thin barrier of his tight, sheer shirt.

Daniel had come to visit Sophia in New York City during his break from medical school in Baltimore. Not knowing anyone and not knowing what to do when your girlfriend was kissing another guy at a party, Daniel took out his iPhone. He pulled up the address book and thumbed through his numbers for someone he had not called for more than two years. He began to feel an increasing sense of urgency about finding her number as the blur of hundreds of friends', colleagues' and family members' names scrolled by his eyes. Then he saw a glimpse of the woman he was searching for: Annie Mercentes.

Daniel's thumb abruptly put the brakes on his iPhone screen. His index finger hovered over her name, just like it had hovered over the last digit of Annie's phone number eight years ago, when he had summoned the courage to ask her out during their senior year at the Ohio State University. Annie was the president of the College Democrats, and with a big election just a few weeks away, she was canvassing the campus to get students registered to vote. She approached Daniel and three of his fraternity brothers, who were in the middle of practicing pass routes for an upcoming flag football tournament, and began asking them if they were registered to vote.

Annie was cute. She had average-size facial features, deep brown eyes and a sparse amount of lip gloss. Maybe it was something about the way she held herself, her confident tone of voice or her passion about politics. She spoke with crisp intent about balanced budgets, foreign policy and a host of other issues, which were clearly lost on Daniel's fraternity brothers. Daniel found her to be magnetic.

That was when one of Daniel's fraternity brothers, partly annoyed that his flag football practice had been interrupted and partly intimidated intellectually, barked a challenge at Annie. "I'm going to run down the field twenty yards, and if you can throw this football all the way down there, then we'll all sign your stupid form."

Daniel began to protest, but Annie quickly retorted, "Well, then, why don't you give me your stupid football?"

The challenger sneered with skepticism as he ran halfheartedly toward a spot twenty yards down the field. When he was about eighteen yards away, Annie squared herself sideways, drew the football behind her left ear and then, in the flash of an eye, whipped around, unleashing a tight spiral toward his right shoulder. When he turned around, one could see a look of terror in his eyes as the rocket Annie had delivered flew through his hands and into his sternum. So with one fraternity brother on one knee, trying to catch his breath, and the other two fraternity brothers signing voter registration forms, Daniel managed to get Annie's phone number. A day later, he mustered the courage to push the last digit of her phone number on his landline, and that kicked off two of the best years of his life.

As midnight struck, the cheers and the sound of cheap plastic kazoos filled the Brooklyn penthouse, and Daniel glanced dispassionately at Sophia, who was now kissing the tight end. That was when Daniel began to wonder how he had ended up with Sophia instead of Annie. Why was he at a pretentious party with people he didn't like, and why was he wearing skinny jeans? Daniel decided that his life had taken some bad turns, and all he wanted to do now was turn toward the only woman he had ever really loved.

He felt that Annie would not want to answer his call, not after his clumsy exit from their relationship two years earlier, but what did he have to lose? While he was filled with questions about his current circumstances, he did know that Annie embodied what he really wanted, and deep down he had known that for a long time. So he decided to act. As Daniel pressed his finger against her name, he reasoned that he could just leave a message, apologize profusely for how he had left things long ago and ask her to call him back. That was why his heart nearly jumped out of his chest when Annie answered her phone.

WISHES DO COME TRUE

We began this book with a simple premise: wishes for happily ever after can come true. We've seen that happily ever after can be hard to find these days, and that is partly attributable to people squandering their three wishes for love on traits in partners that don't really contribute toward relationships that are satisfying and stable. Yet despite some of the depressing statistics about dating and marriage, I am still convinced after reading thousands of research reports and critically considering their collective implications that happily ever is indeed a possibility, and that people who want this ending to their love story should settle for nothing less. Fairy-tale endings *are* possible. It's just that happily ever after doesn't happen with the swish of a wand or a magic spell. Wishes come true when people use their wishes well and then *act* in ways that make those wishes come to fruition.

One of the morals of most fairy tales, something sometimes forgotten in the midst of feel-good romance, is that the protagonist's wishes for love come true only when he or she takes some action to make those wishes come true. Fairy tales often start with the lonely protagonist longing for enduring love, and just when someone promising comes waltzing into the protagonist's life, he or she is confronted with a challenge. It doesn't really matter whether the challenge is Cinderella losing her slipper or a mermaid losing her voice. What matters is that the challenge to enduring love is overcome when two things happen: the protagonist gains insight into a hidden mystery and he or she takes heroic action.

You have already made great strides toward gaining insight into the mystery of romantic love by simply deciding to read a book about the science of partner selection. We've seen how science can provide new insights into why some people don't find the enduring love they want. In real life, psychologists know that people achieve meaningful change when they begin to see what a better future would look like and then take action to make that desired future become a reality. In the preceding chapters of this book, we reviewed the science that can provide insight about how to select partners with traits that greatly improve the chances of finding enduring love. In this chapter, I'll tell you about some advances from psychotherapy research that can help you turn the knowledge you have gained about relationship science into a concrete plan of action that gives you a chance to make meaningful changes in your partner selection and relationships.

ACTIVATING YOUR WISHES

Building on previous behavioral therapy research and cutting-edge research, Dr. Carl Lejuez, a psychology professor and his colleagues at the University of Maryland, have developed a straightforward and effective psychological intervention called "behavioral activation." Behavioral activation places the focus on what people actually do, instead of on the past or their feelings about things. I've been impressed by how firmly the treatment is grounded in sound psychological science and by how effective it has been in clinical trials. Behavioral activation is relatively easy to understand, and the intervention has helped hundreds of people overcome serious problems, such as depression, substance abuse and PTSD.

The stories people tell me about their relationship concerns—whether it's realizing that they keep dating the same dysfunctional types of partners or feeling stuck when it comes to pursuing the kinds of partners that would be more ideal for what they want to accomplish in their romantic relationships—have led me to believe that an intervention like behavioral activation might prove helpful. People's relationship concerns may actually stem from attachment issues, feelings of emotional distress or unhelpful beliefs about themselves or others, and what they often need to do is just start doing what they know is the best thing for them. Many times in life we know exactly what we should be doing, but what holds us back is the fear of moving forward into uncharted territory, even if it's something that we think we really want in our lives.

In the behavioral activation framework, people are thought to become unhappy with an aspect of their life because they have slipped into acting in ways that are incongruent with what they really value in life. This disconnect between what they really value or wish for in their life and how they actually act makes people feel stuck, which can lead to sadness, anxiety or unhealthy ways of trying to escape (e.g., subconsciously choosing dead-end relationships). Although the behavioral activation approach does not discount past experience, feelings or unhelpful thoughts, the focus is sharply on changing how people act on a daily basis.

Dr. Lejuez suggests that when people begin doing things that move them toward their goals, they begin to feel a sense optimism and increased self-worth, and they don't have as much time to engage in destructive behaviors. A great aspect of behavioral activation is that in addition to decreasing dysfunction, it increases positive functioning. This emphasis on increasing good behaviors to trump negative life circumstances makes it an excellent framework for helping people translate their insights about how to spend their three wishes wisely into actions that will actually help them select better romantic partners.

If what you ultimately want is to find a long-term relationship that is satisfying and stable, and you're ready to start pursuing that outcome, then behavioral activation can help you:

1. Clarify your ultimate goal.

2. Diagnose what you usually wish for.

3. Focus your three wishes on the traits you really want in a partner.

4. Devise a structured plan of action to act on your three wishes.

5. Evaluate your progress.

In the next section, I'll describe the key steps in this process.

KEY STEPS TO BEHAVIORAL ACTIVATION

1. Clarify Your Ultimate Goal

Here's an important question to consider before moving forward. What do you want from your love life? As we've seen throughout this book, cultural and social pressure can influence our beliefs about romantic relationships, which suggests that individuals should consider whether they really want an "ever after." Some people feel that they are too young for a lifelong commitment, others are not so young and realize that they just really enjoy being single and some people decide that they need some time to work on their personal lives before bringing romantic partners into the picture. The point is that the ultimate goal for your love life does not have to be what everyone else wants.

We saw in previous chapters that the goal of marriage has changed dramatically since the romantic era. Until then, humans lived for thousands of years with the constant threat of starvation, thirst and epidemic disease. With average life expectancies under forty years of age and a 33 percent chance that your children would not survive to age thirty-five, mate selection was narrowly focused on the ultimate goal of survival. Understandably, humans came to value two traits when basic needs and longevity were far from guaranteed: partners with access to resources and partners who looked healthy. These traits were valued for thousands of years, across hundreds of generations, which means that the rapid increase in life expectancy and the vast improvement in the odds of reproductive success over the past 150 years had to give rise to a dramatic shift in the rules of the mating game.

However, we've seen that most people continue to spend two of their three wishes for traits on physical attractiveness and wealth, despite getting little to no return on their investment in these two traits when it comes to reproductive fitness, relationship satisfaction and relationship stability. All species, including humans, tend to retain mechanisms of survival long after those mechanisms have lost their usefulness. The preference for mates who are physically attractive and who have resources can be thought of in this way, because privileging these two characteristics made sense for most of human history. However, given the rapid changes in our mating environment, our mate selection behaviors are a bit like wisdom teeth, a feature that was once useful but is now unnecessary, can cause pain and is often in need of removal.

So, if your ultimate goal is to find enduring love, then you can move on to the next step, which is identifying your partner selection patterns from previous relationships.

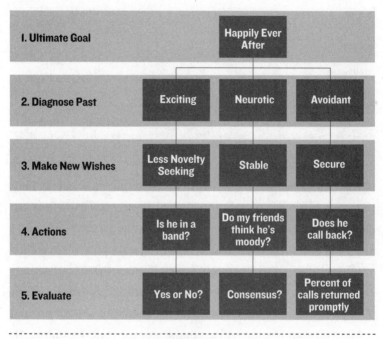

FIGURE 10.1

An overview of behavioral activation for partner selection.

2. Identify Your Partner Selection Patterns

Once you are clear about your ultimate goal, take a few minutes to do an assessment of your past relationship partners, which might help clarify why things did not always work out in past relationships.

Think about the last three people you dated or wanted to date. Write their initials in the far left-hand column. Using the same rating scales from Chapter 7 for personality and Chapter 8 for attachment styles (see the note beneath the sample table), rate those former partners on novelty seeking, neuroticism and agreeableness, and then identify their attachment style. Here is a sample table:

Attracted to:	Novelty Seeking	Neuroticism	Agreeableness	Attachment
Initials:				
Initials:				
Initials:				

Note: Rate personality traits on a scale of 1 (strongly disagree) to 7 (strongly agree). Attachment style categories are secure, anxious and avoidant. Go to tytashiro.net for additional information.

After you have completed your assessment of past relationship partners, step back and think about the patterns you see in the partners you selected. Incorporating knowledge gained from previous chapters, take a moment to consider whether the partners you choose give you the best chance of finding satisfying and stable relationships.

It's also worthwhile to rate yourself on all these traits and to consider why you choose the types of partners that you do. How have your past partners' traits rewarded you (e.g., novelty seekers are fun) or kept you away from something that scares you (e.g., commitment)? This is no easy task, because sometimes it requires taking a closer look at personal shortcomings, and that can be tough on our self-worth. It's easy for any of us to discern someone else's tendency to choose the wrong partners, but it's more difficult to ask ourselves why we choose the wrong partners for ourselves.

This exercise in introspection might lead you to conclude that you need to make some changes in what you wish for in romantic partners, but you might also decide that you want to wish for something that doesn't necessarily fit with the science we reviewed earlier in the book. Based on your personal preferences, you might decide that you really need someone who is high on novelty seeking or a bit avoidantly attached. Doing so does not necessarily mean that your relationships will be doomed, but it's also important to think about what risks that presents and how a couple can deal effectively with those potential risks to relationship satisfaction or stability. The point is to be aware of what you are doing when you select partners and to be honest with yourself about the risks that come with some of your preferences.

3. Make Your Wishes

Long-term relationship satisfaction and relationship stability come from adding a healthy dose of knowledge and intelligent analysis to the intuitive feeling that someone might be something special. One of the first concepts we examined was how much people can reasonably wish for before it becomes mathematically impossible for them to find the ideal partners they are seeking. If one makes three wishes for traits for a potential partner in the seventieth percentile (e.g., a seven out of ten on looks), the probability of finding someone with those traits is only 30 percent. So the question became how those precious wishes should be spent.

Although you need to prioritize your wishes and become crystal clear about your top three wishes, for the sake of this exercise, forget for a moment that you get only three wishes. Indulge yourself by listing ten wishes for traits in potential romantic partners. It's fine to include a few wishes that you know don't usually contribute to finding happily ever after (e.g., physical attractiveness). Be honest with yourself. Once you've made a list, go back and rank order the traits from most important (1) to least important (10). Here is a sample list.

Traits. I'm Wishing for Someone Who:	Rank Order
A. Is very agreeable	1
B. Has at least average emotional stability	4
C. Is securely attached	2
D. Has high novelty seeking (but not too high)	3
E. Capitalizes when I share good news	6
F. Is intelligent	5
G. Is cute	8
H. Does not blame me for everything	7
I. Is unlikely to withdraw in a relationship	9
J. Appreciates good music	10

The purpose of this exercise is to think critically about some of the conflicting wishes you harbor during partner selection. Ranking our wishes makes it more likely that we will direct our attention toward the traits that really matter and watch out for traits that we might intuitively desire but that we intellectually know aren't good for us in the long run.

4.   Design a Plan of Action

Now we're going to select some actions, things you will actually do, that are consistent with your top three wishes. Think about smaller goals that have some degree of difficulty, that make you just a little bit uncomfortable. The degree of difficulty and the size of the smaller goals can be thought of in terms of physically stretching your muscles: you want to push yourself to achieve a little bit of tension and discomfort, but you don't want to stretch too far, as that would make the exercise painful.

In Chapter 6, we reviewed why people tend to make very poor decisions when faced with a big problem that has a "yes or no" answer. The key to avoiding poor decisions is to look at smaller parts of the problem, rather than the problem as a whole, which, in the context of partner selection, means making judgments about the traits that make up a whole person. Once those traits are accurately assessed, it's possible to make a more informed decision about the whole picture, that is, whether a partner is likely to provide a satisfying and stable relationship.

When it comes to taking action on big goals, people oftentimes meet with limited progress, because they focus mostly on the larger goal, instead of breaking it down into smaller goals, which can be accomplished on the way to the bigger success. Finding a happy and enduring relationship is one of the biggest goals people pursue in their lifetime, and breaking up the task of finding a partner into smaller goals can improve your chances of success because the task becomes more manageable.

Take the following example of someone whose last three boyfriends have cheated on her. When evaluating her past relationships, she realizes that she tends to date guys who average about a seven on novelty seeking, which might explain their propensity to cheat. Thinking beyond the last three guys she dated, she realizes that she has a weak spot for guys who play the bass guitar in bands and that sleepovers tend to occur after first meeting them. So in addition to having her friends eventually rate a new guy on novelty seeking, she decides to devise two clear-cut goals for future actions: to say no for now to dating guys who are in bands and to triple the time before a sleepover occurs. Although these three smaller goals will not guarantee that she finds a guy with more impulse control, most outside observers of her relationship patterns would probably say that these are a step in the right direction for now. Here is how her goals look when arranged in a table.

First Wish = Someone with more impulse control (less novelty seeking)

Actions Consistent with this Wish Coming True	Enjoyment (0–10)	Importance (0–10)
1. Don't date guys in a band	3	7
2. Wait until at least the third date before sleeping over	5	9

She then rates each goal on her anticipated enjoyment doing it and on its importance to her. Her ratings indicate that she's going to miss dating bass guitarists, but that she knows for now, it's important to take a break from dating them. She loves talking with her girlfriends about relationships, and so talking about their ratings of her future partner's novelty seeking will probably be enjoyable and important. As we see here, not all the small steps you take toward your wishes coming true are enjoyable. Having both enjoyable and not so enjoyable goals is probably the best combination.

Now take one of your wishes and come up with three things you can do that would be consistent with increasing the chances of that wish coming true. Eventually, do this for all your wishes and then place your behavioral activation plan somewhere where you will see it every day.

5.   Track Your Small Victories

Share your goals with some trusted confidants who can provide much-needed encouragement along the way. Avoid friends who will be critical or who will want to micromanage the process, because you probably put enough pressure on yourself. Pick people who will generally encourage your progress and who can gently help you brainstorm about roadblocks that seem to trip you up. Although change is not always enjoyable at the beginning, many people eventually become encouraged by seeing their incremental progress. As you start racking up successful changes, it's important to reward yourself.

Behavioral activation works because it rewards your small victories, whether the reward is seeing your progress on a spreadsheet, hearing encouraging remarks from friends, or finding that these changes actually yield different kinds of partners and relationships. Going from "I really should..." to actually taking action is not easy. You have to stay persistent and stick with your plans, and at times you may have to revise those plans, but hopefully, you will begin to see how a more structured approach like behavioral activation can bridge the distance between your old ways of choosing partners and your new way of choosing partners you can feel good about. With a smart plan, persistent effort and some supportive friends, you can begin to see the trajectory of your love story change.

FINDING YOUR FLOW

By setting goals to act in ways that are congruent with your values (e.g., being a giving partner, a nurturing parent), your pursuit of fulfilling your wishes becomes more focused. Choosing partners who are more in line with helping you achieve your long-term goals will likely lead you to partners who treat you better and relationship experiences that are more gratifying. This cycle of acting in ways that are congruent with your long-term goals in relationships, and then having those actions reinforced by better partners who treat you well, can increase the amount of positive feelings you experience and give you a more hopeful outlook on your love life in general.

Although the early stages of incorporating behavioral activation can be effortful, with consistent practice, the process of recognizing partner selection patterns that have produced unhappy or unstable relationships will become more automatic. By making it a habit to think critically about potential partners, you will find yourself focusing on the three wishes you know are good for you and you might find it easier to take action with potential partners who fit your three wishes. Of course, incorporating behavioral activation with the help of a trained psychotherapist, or at least support from friends who are not afraid to show some tough love, can facilitate your progress.

You will find that the knowledge you have about how to wish for a great partner can be translated into success through a combination of identifying your key values for your romantic relationships, setting specific behavioral goals that are in line with those values and having the discipline to track your progress toward a worthy goal: satisfying and reliable relationships.

BE BRAVE

Daniel did not expect Annie to pick up the phone. They hadn't spoken in two years, not since he flipped out about being so deeply in love with someone who was twenty-four years old, then decided that they needed "to see other people and try new things," in the process devastating Annie's faith in his willingness to be there for her. The words to say rolled through his mind so quickly that he could not grab hold of a single useful thing to say. Annie broke the audible silence.

"You're surprised that I answered?"

"Yes. Very surprised."

"I'm at a New Year's party and it sucks."

"Me too."

"Daniel, I wish you were here."

"I would do anything to be with you in Palo Alto."

"I'm actually in Brooklyn for the weekend. . . ."

A few moments later, Daniel and Annie were running toward the carousel near the Manhattan Bridge. Daniel's legs burned from the friction created by those stupid skinny jeans. He felt his chest chafing on the synthetic fabrics of his semi-glossy silver shirt. The wind was biting, yet he was overcome with an absurd desire to cast away those clothes. To run free from what had been a foolish past two years of his life. He looked silly because he was not himself. He had bought into a facade, some disingenuous set of beliefs that Annie never would have tolerated, much less encouraged.

That was when the demons that had sent him down this misguided path in the first place began climbing into his consciousness, threatening to derail his journey toward his destination. How could someone so kind, secure and reasonable want to run to *him?* After he broke her heart two years ago, for hopes and wishes that were purely foolish, maybe he didn't deserve her trust and affection. In this moment of self-doubt, Daniel teetered between giving in to the damning demons of self-doubt and embracing the promising hope that comes with knowing your worth.

None of us are perfect. None of us embody all the desirable traits described in this book. After all, the probabilities are against that happening. We all make mistakes, and sometimes we make big mistakes, but for someone in Annie's situation, the question becomes whether a partner's mistakes are truly mistakes, byproducts of tough circumstances or aberrations in behavior. Alternatively, other mistakes may be part of a larger pattern of behavior, and the same repeated mistake over time eventually becomes a trait.

Daniel was extremely kind, was emotionally stable and was very high in novelty seeking, and he possessed a moderately avoidant attachment style. During the two years they dated, Annie had observed that he did not default to blaming her for problems, never demanded more than she could give and never withdrew from matters that were important to her in the relationship. He was always so proud of what she had accomplished, encouraged her success and had full faith in her future.

Ultimately, it was his capacity to love her so deeply that activated Daniel's irrational fear that Annie would not love him in return. At some subliminal level, Daniel worried that he was not worthy of a love like Annie's and that it was just a matter of time before she figured it out. So he fled to pursue medical school in Baltimore, while Annie went west for graduate studies at Stanford. Annie would have discussed a compromise and might have even sacrificed some of her career ambitions to be with Daniel, but he had never allowed the discussion to happen. For that, he was deeply sorry.

Stories like Daniel and Annie's, which begin so beautifully, can end in tragedy when the protagonists drift too far from their virtues or fail to act bravely during crucial junctures. Good people can feel the allure of beauty, prestige or power. If those critical moments occur when we are a little weak or a little lonely, the choices we make about lifelong partners can be devastating to our hopes. Although Daniel was near the top of his medical school class, he found himself drifting from who he really was without Annie as an anchor. We know that faith in the swishes of wands for love to appear or magical elixirs to cure us of our demons are not the answers to finding enduring love. You *create* your version of happily ever after by wishing wisely for great partners and then having the courage to trust your ability to love well and to be loved in return.

Daniel and Annie had wished for great partners, had found what they were looking for and then had lost it. Whether it was fate or not that brought both of them to Brooklyn that night is not for me to decide, but what is certain is that they were each faced with important decisions to make if their wishes were to come true. Daniel needed to wash himself clean of his misguided detour and believe in the permanence of Annie's love. Annie needed to reach a measured decision and then have the virtue to forgive. They both found the courage to act as needed, and so when Daniel ran toward Annie, who stood illuminated by the bright lights of the carousel, he saw a woman standing before him who was everything he could wish for.

BIBLIOGRAPHY

CHAPTER I

Berndt, T. J. "Friendship Quality and Social Development." *Current Directions in Psychological Science* 11 (2002): 7–10.

Berscheid, E. "The Greening of Relationship Science." *American Psychologist* 54 (1999): 260–66.

Berscheid, E. "Love in the Fourth Dimension." *Annual Review of Psychology* 61 (2010): 1–25.

Christensen, A., and C. L. Heavey. "Interventions for Couples." Annual Review of Psychology 50 (1999): 165–90.

Coontz, Stephanie. *Marriage, A History: How Love Conquered Marriage.* New York: Penguin, 2006.

Fehr, B., and J. A. Russell. "The Concept of Love Viewed from a Prototype Perspective." *Journal of Personality and Social Psychology* 60 (1991): 425–38.

Franiuk, R., D. Cohen, and E. M. Pomerantz. "Implicit Theories of Relationships: Implications for Relationship Satisfaction and Longevity." *Personal Relationships* 9 (2002): 345–67.

Holmes B., and K. Johnson. "Where Fantasy Meets Reality: Media Exposure, Relationship Beliefs and Standards, and the Moderating Effect of a Current Relationship." Chap. 6 in *Social Psychology: New Research.* Hauppauge, NY: Nova Science, 2009.

Huston, T. L., J. P. Caughlin, R. M. Houts, S. E. Smith, and L. J. George. "The Connubial Crucible: Newlywed Years as Predictors of Marital Delight, Distress, and Divorce." *Journal of Personality and Social Psychology* 80 (2001): 237–52.

Karney, B. R, and T. N. Bradbury. "The Longitudinal Course of Marital Quality and Stability: A Review of Theory, Methods, and Research." *Psychological Bulletin* 118 (1995): 3–34.

Levine, R., S. Sato, T. Hashimoto, and J. Verma. "Love and Marriage in Eleven Cultures." *Journal of Cross-Cultural Psychology* 26 (1995): 554–71.

Loving, T. J., E. E. Crockett, and A. A. Paxson. "Passionate Love and Relationship Thinkers: Experimental Evidence for Acute Cortisol Elevations in Women." *Psychoneuroendocrinology* 34 (2009): 939–46.

Martin, T. C., and L. L. Bumpass. "Recent Trends in Marital Disruption." *Demography* 26 (1989): 37–51.

McAdams, D. P., and B. D. Olson. "Personality Development: Continuity and Change over the Life Course." *Annual Review of Psychology* 61 (2010): 517–42.

Meyers, S. A., and E. Berscheid. "The Language of Love: The Difference a Preposition Makes." *Personality and Social Psychology Bulletin* 23 (1997): 347–62.

Pardun, Carol J. "Romancing the Script: Identifying the Romantic Agenda in Top-Grossing Movies." Chap. 10 in *Sexual Teens, Sexual Media: Investigating Media's Influence on Adolescent Sexuality.* New York: Routledge, 2002.

Peplau, L. A. "Human Sexuality." *Current Directions in Psychological Science* 12 (2003): 37–40.

Propp, Vladimir. *Morphology of the Folktale.* Translated by Laurence Scott. Austin: University of Texas Press, 1971.

Rideout, V. J., U. G. Foehr, and D. F. Roberts. *Generation M2: Media in the Lives of 8- to 18-Year-Olds.* A Kaiser Family Foundation Study, 2010.

Tanner, L. R., S. A. Haddock, T. S. Zimmerman, and L. K. Lund. "Images of Couples and Families in Disney Feature-Length Animated Films." *American Journal of Family Therapy* 31 (2003): 355–73.

Tashiro, T., and P. Frazier. "I'll Never Be in a Relationship Like That Again: Personal Growth Following Relationship Dissolution." *Personal Relationships* 10 (2003): 113–28.

Truman, J., and M. Rand. (2010). *Criminal Victimization.* Bureau of Justice Statistics. Accessed February 14, 2012. www.bjs.ojp.usdoj.gov/content/pub/pdf/cv09.pdf.

U.S. Fire Administration Fire Estimates. (2010). Accessed February 14, 2012. www.usfa.dhs.gov/statistics/estimates/index.shtm.

Whitehead, B., and D. Popenoe. "Singles Seek Soul Mates for Marriage." (2001). Accessed February 14, 2012. www.gallup.com/poll/4552/Singles-Seek-Soul-Mates-Marriage.aspx.

CHAPTER 2

Acevedo, B. P., and A. Aron. "Does a Long-Term Relationship Kill Romantic Love?" *Review of General Psychology* 13 (2009): 59.

Aron, A., E. N. Aron, and D. Smollan. "Inclusion of Other in the Self Scale and the Structure of Interpersonal Closeness." *Journal of Personality and Social Psychology* 63 (1992): 596–612.

Caspi, A., B. W. Roberts, and R. L. Shiner. "Personality Development: Stability and Change." *Annual Review Psychology* 56 (2005): 453–84.

Current Population Survey: Annual Social and Economic Supplement. Accessed February 14, 2012. www.census.gov/hhes/www/cpstables/032011/perinc/new11_001.htm.

Current Population Survey: Annual Social and Economic Supplement: Accessed February 14, 2012. www.pubdb3.census.gov/macro/032006/perinc/new03_145.htm.

Fincham, F. D., G. T. Harold, and S. Gano-Phillips. "The Longitudinal Association Between Attributions and Marital Satisfaction: Direction of Effects and Role of Efficacy Expectations." *Journal of Family Psychology* 14 (2000): 267.

Fletcher, G. J. O., and P. S. G. Kerr. "Through the Eyes of Love: Reality and Illusion in Intimate Relationships." *Psychological Bulletin* 136 (2010): 627–58.

Gottman, J. M., and R. W. Levenson. "A Two-Factor Model for Predicting When a Couple Will Divorce: Exploratory Analyses Using 14-Year Longitudinal Data*." *Family Process* 41 (2002): 83–96.

Griffin, A. M., and J. H. Langlois. "Stereotype Directionality and Attractiveness Stereotyping: Is Beauty Good or Is Ugly Bad?" *Social Cognition* 24 (2006): 187–206.

Jones, J. M. "Record High 40% of Americans Identify as Independents in '11." (January 9, 2012). Accessed February 14. 2012. www.gallup.com/poll/151943/Record-High-Americans-Identify-Independents.aspx.

Kahneman, D. "Maps of Bounded Rationality: Psychology for Behavioral Economics." *The American Economic Review* 93 (2003): 1449–75.

Kelley, H. H., E. Berscheid, A. Christensen, J. H. Harvey, T. L. Huston, G. Levinger, E. McClintock, L. A. Peplau, and D. R. Peterson. *Close Relationships*. New York: Freeman, 1983.

Lykken, D. T., and A. Tellegen. "Is Human Mating Adventitious or the Result of Lawful Choice? A Twin Study of Mate Selection." *Journal of Personality and Social Psychology* 65 (1993): 56–68.

McDowell, M. A., C. D. Fryar, C. L. Ogden, and K. M. Flegal. "Anthropometric Reference Data for Children and Adults: United States 2003–2006." *National Health Statistics Reports* 10 (2008). Accessed February 14, 2012. www.cdc.gov/nchs/data/nhsr/nhsr010.pdf

Murray, S. L., and J. G. Holmes. "A Leap of Faith? Positive Illusions in Romantic Relationships." *Personality and Social Psychology Bulletin* 23 (1997): 586–604.

Ozer, D. J., and V. Benet-Martínez. "Personality and the Prediction of Consequential Outcomes." *Annual Review of Psychology* 57 (2006): 401–21.

Pew Forum on Religion and Public Life: U.S. Religious Landscape Survey. Accessed February 14, 2012. www.religions.pewforum.org/pdf/report-religious-landscape-study-chapter-3.pdf.

Saucier, G. "Mini-Markers: A Brief Version of Goldberg's Unipolar Big-Five Markers." *Journal of Personality Assessment* 63 (1994): 506–16.

Tashiro, T., and P. Frazier. "The Casual Effects of Emotion on Couples." *Journal of Counseling Psychology* 54 (2007): 409–22.

CHAPTER 3

Berscheid, Ellen, Karen Dion, Elaine Walster, and G. William Walster. "Physical Attractiveness and Dating Choice: A Test of the Matching Hypothesis." *Journal of Experimental Social Psychology* 7, no. 2 (1971): 173–89.

Boivin, Jacky, Laura Bunting, John A. Collins, and Karl G. Nygren. "International Estimates of Infertility Prevalence and Treatment-Seeking: Potential Need and Demand for Infertility Medical Care." *Human Reproduction* 22, no. 6 (2007): 1506–12.

Buss, David M. "The Great Struggles of Life: Darwin and the Emergence of Evolutionary Psychology." *American Psychologist* 64, no. 2 (2009): 140.

Buss, David M. "How Can Evolutionary Psychology Successfully Explain Personality and Individual Differences?" *Perspectives on Psychological Science* 4, no. 4 (2009): 359–66.

Confer, Jaime C., Judith A. Easton, Diana S. Fleischman, Cari D. Goetz, David M. G. Lewis, Carin Perilloux, and David M. Buss. "Evolutionary Psychology: Controversies, Questions, Prospects, and Limitations." *American Psychologist* 65, no. 2 (2010): 110.

Coontz, Stephanie. *Marriage, A History: How Love Conquered Marriage.* New York: Penguin, 2006.

Coontz, Stephanie. "The World Historical Transformation of Marriage." *Journal of Marriage and Family* 66, no. 4 (2004): 974–79.

Doumic, René. *George Sand: Some Aspects of Her Life and Writings.* Translated by Alys Hallard. Gloucester: Dodo Press, 2009.

Feingold, Alan. "Gender Differences in Mate Selection Preferences: A Test of the Parental Investment Model." *Psychological Bulletin* 112, no. 1 (1992): 125.

Floud, Roderick, Robert W. Fogel, Bernard Harris, and Sok Chul Hong. *The Changing Body: Health, Nutrition, and Human Development in the Western World since 1700.* Cambridge: Cambridge University Press, 2011.

Gangestad, Steven W., and Jeffry A. Simpson. "The Evolution of Human Mating: Trade-offs and Strategic Pluralism." *Behavioral and Brain Sciences* 23, no. 4 (2000): 573–87.

Goodfriend, Wind, and Christopher R. Agnew. "Sunken Costs and Desired Plans: Examining Different Types of Investments in Close Relationships." *Personality and Social Psychology Bulletin* 34, no. 12 (2008): 1639–52.

The Human Mortality Database. The Department of Demography at the University of California, Berkeley, and at the Max Planck Institute for Demographic Research in Rostock. www.mortality.org/.

Infertility FAQs. Accessed on April 19, 2012. www.cdc.gov/reproductivehealth/Infertility.

Johansson, Klara, and Mattias Lindgren. November 10, 2011. Documentation for Life Expectancy at Birth (years) for Countries and Territories.

Kundera, Milan. *The Unbearable Lightness of Being.* New York: Harper, 2004.

Li, Norman P., J. Michael Bailey, Douglas T. Kenrick, and Joan A. W. Linsenmeier. "The Necessities and Luxuries of Mate Preferences: Testing the Tradeoffs." *Journal of Personality and Social Psychology* 82, no. 6 (2002): 947.

Lindgren, Mattias. May 28, 2008. Documentation for GDP Per Capita by Purchasing Power Parities for Sub-National Units.

Maslow, Abraham H. "Hierarchy of Needs in a Theory of Human Motivation." In *Motivation and Personality,* 2nd ed. New York: Harper & Row, 1970.

Miller, William R., and Stephen P. Rollnick. *Motivational Interviewing: Preparing People for Change.* New York: Guilford Press, 2002.

Ombelet, Willem, Ian Cooke, Silke Dyer, Gamal Serour, and Paul Devroey. "Infertility and the Provision of Infertility Medical Services in Developing Countries." *Human Reproduction Update* 14, no. 6 (2008): 605–21.

Persson, Hans, Bertil Wikman, and Birgitta Strandvik. "Frédéric Chopin—the Man, His Music and His Illness." *Przegla̧d lekarski* 62, no. 6 (2005): 321.

Réale, Denis, Niels J. Dingemanse, Anahita J. N. Kazem, and Jonathan Wright. "Evolutionary and Ecological Approaches to the Study of Personality." *Philosophical Transactions of the Royal Society B: Biological Sciences* 365, no. 1560 (2010): 3937–46.

Watson, David, Eva C. Klohnen, Alex Casillas, Ericka Nus Simms, Jeffrey Haig, and Diane S. Berry. "Match Makers and Deal Breakers: Analyses of Assortative Mating in Newlywed Couples." *Journal of Personality* 72, no. 5 (2004): 1029–68.

CHAPTER 4

Anderson, Cameron, Oliver P. John, Dacher Keltner, and Ann M. Kring. "Who Attains Social Status? Effects of Personality and Physical Attractiveness in Social Groups." *Journal of Personality and Social Psychology* 81, no. 1 (2001): 116.

Berry, Diane S. "Attractiveness, Attraction, and Sexual Selection: Evolutionary Perspectives on the Form and Function of Physical Attractiveness." *Advances in Experimental Social Psychology* 32 (2000): 273–342.

Dion, Karen K., and Ellen Berscheid. "Physical Attractiveness and Peer Perception among Children." *Sociometry* 37, no. 1 (1974): 1–12.

Dion, Karen K., Ellen Berscheid, and Elaine Walster. "What Is Beautiful Is Good." *Journal of Personality and Social Psychology* 24, no. 3 (1972): 285.

Eagly, Alice H., Richard D. Ashmore, Mona G. Makhijani, and Laura C. Longo. "What Is Beautiful Is Good, but . . . : A Meta-Analytic Review of Research on the Physical Attractiveness Stereotype." *Psychological Bulletin* 110, no. 1 (1991): 109.

Feingold, Alan. "Good-Looking People Are Not What We Think." *Psychological Bulletin* 111, no. 2 (1992): 304.

Fink, Bernhard, and Ian Penton-Voak. "Evolutionary Psychology of Facial Attractiveness." *Current Directions in Psychological Science* 11, no. 5 (2002): 154–58.

Gangestad, Steven W., and Glenn J. Scheyd. "The Evolution of Human Physical Attractiveness." *Annual Review of Anthropology* 34 (2005): 523–48.

Haidt, Jonathan. "The Emotional Dog and Its Rational Tail: A Social Intuitionist Approach to Moral Judgment." *Psychological Review* 108, no. 4 (2001): 814.

Judge, Timothy A., Charlice Hurst, and Lauren S. Simon. "Does It Pay to Be Smart, Attractive, or Confident (Or All Three)? Relationships among General Mental Ability, Physical Attractiveness, Core Self-Evaluations, and Income." *Journal of Applied Psychology* 94, no. 3 (2009): 742.

Kahneman, Daniel. "A Perspective on Judgment and Choice: Mapping Bounded Rationality." *American Psychologist* 58, no. 9 (2003): 697.

Kahneman, Daniel, and Amos Tversky. "Prospect Theory: An Analysis of Decision under Risk." *Econometrica* 47, no. 2 (1979): 263–92.

Langlois, Judith H., Lisa Kalakanis, Adam J. Rubenstein, Andrea Larson, Monica Hallam, and Monica Smoot. "Maxims or Myths of Beauty? A Meta-Analytic and Theoretical Review." *Psychological Bulletin* 126, no. 3 (2000): 390.

Langlois, Judith H., and Cookie Stephan. "The Effects of Physical Attractiveness and Ethnicity on Children's Behavioral Attributions and Peer Preferences." *Child Development* 48 (1977): 1694–98.

Marlowe, Frank, and Adam Wetsman. "Preferred Waist-to-Hip Ratio and Ecology." *Personality and Individual Differences* 30, no. 3 (2001): 481–89.

McNulty, James K., Lisa A. Neff, and Benjamin R. Karney. "Beyond Initial Attraction: Physical Attractiveness in Newlywed Marriage." *Journal of Family Psychology* 22, no. 1 (2008): 135.

Petty, Richard E., Duane T. Wegener, and Leandre R. Fabrigar. "Attitudes and Attitude Change." *Annual Review of Psychology* 48, no. 1 (1997): 609–47.

Rhodes, Gillian. "The Evolutionary Psychology of Facial Beauty." *Annual Review of Psychology* 57 (2006): 199–226.

Snyder, Mark, Elizabeth D. Tanke, and Ellen Berscheid. "Social Perception and Interpersonal Behavior: On the Self-Fulfilling Nature of Social Stereotypes." *Journal of Personality and Social Psychology* 35, no. 9 (1977): 656.

Stephan, Cookie White, and Judith H. Langlois. "Baby Beautiful: Adult Attributions of Infant Competence as a Function of Infant Attractiveness." *Child Development* 55 (1984): 576–85.

Weeden, Jason, and John Sabini. "Physical Attractiveness and Health in Western Societies: A Review." *Psychological Bulletin* 131, no. 5 (2005): 635.

CHAPTER 5

Americans' Access to Basic Necessities Gradually Improving. (n.d.). Retrieved from www.gallup.com/poll/154073/americans-access-basic-necessities-gradually-improving.aspx.

Arndt, Jamie, Sheldon Solomon, Tim Kasser, and Kennon M. Sheldon. "The Urge to Splurge: A Terror Management Account of Materialism and Consumer Behavior." *Journal of Consumer Psychology* 14, no. 3 (2004): 198–212.

Braveman, Paula A., Catherine Cubbin, Susan Egerter, David R. Williams, and Elsie Pamuk. "Socioeconomic Disparities in Health in the United States: What the Patterns Tell Us." *American Journal of Public Health* 100, no. S1 (2010): S186–S196.

Conger, Rand D., Ming Cui, Chalandra M. Bryant, and Glen H. Elder Jr. "Competence in Early Adult Romantic Relationships: A Developmental Perspective on Family Influences." *Journal of Personality and Social Psychology* 79, no. 2 (2000): 224.

Conger, Rand D., and M. Brent Donnellan. "An Interactionist Perspective on the Socioeconomic Context of Human Development." *Annual Review of Psychology* 58 (2007): 175–99.

DeNavas-Walt, Carmen, Bernadette D. Proctor, and Jessica C. Smith. Income Poverty, and Health Insurance Coverage in the United States: *2011 U.S. Census Bureau, Current Population Reports.* Washington D.C.: U.S. Government Printing Office (2012): 60.243

Diener, Ed, and Robert Biswas-Diener. "Will Money Increase Subjective Well-Being?" *Social Indicators Research* 57, no. 2 (2002): 119–69.

Easterlin, Richard A. "Lost in Transition: Life Satisfaction on the Road to Capitalism." *Journal of Economic Behavior & Organization* 71, no. 2 (2009): 130–45.

Haidt, Jonathan. *The Happiness Hypothesis: Finding Modern Truth in Ancient Wisdom.* New York: Basic Books, 2005.

Howell, Ryan T., and Colleen J. Howell. "The Relation of Economic Status to Subjective Well-Being in Developing Countries: A Meta-Analysis." *Psychological Bulletin* 134, no. 4 (2008): 536.

Kahneman, Daniel, and Angus Deaton. "High Income Improves Evaluation of Life but not Emotional Well-Being." *Proceedings of the National Academy of Sciences* 107, no. 38 (2010): 16489–93.

Kasser, Tim, and Allen D. Kanner, eds. *Psychology and Consumer Culture: The Struggle for a Good Life in a Materialistic World.* Washington, D.C.: American Psychological Association, 2004.

Kim, Jeounghee. "A Diverging Trend in Marital Dissolution by Income Status." *Journal of Divorce & Remarriage* 51, no. 7 (2010): 396–412.

Luthar, Suniya S., and Bronwyn E. Becker. "Privileged But Pressured? A Study of Affluent Youth." *Child Development* 73, no. 5 (2003): 1593–610.

National Occupational Employment and Wage Estimates, May 2011. United States. Accessed on May 29, 2011. www.bls.gov/oes/current/oes_nat.htm.

Mirvis, David M., and David E. Bloom. "Population Health and Economic Development in the United States." *JAMA* 300, no. 1 (2008): 93–95.

Steger, Michael F., Todd B. Kashdan, and Shigehiro Oishi. "Being Good by Doing Good: Daily Eudaimonic Activity and Well-Being." *Journal of Research in Personality* 42, no. 1 (2008): 22–42.

Stuckler, David, Sanjay Basu, Marc Suhrcke, Adam Coutts, and Martin McKee. "The Public Health Effect of Economic Crises and Alternative Policy Responses in Europe: An Empirical Analysis." *The Lancet* 374, no. 9686 (2009): 315–23.

White, Lynn, and Stacy J. Rogers. "Economic Circumstances and Family Outcomes: A Review of the 1990s." *Journal of Marriage and Family* 62, no. 4 (2004): 1035–51.

CHAPTER 6

Agnew, Christopher R., Timothy J. Loving, and Stephen M. Drigotas. "Substituting the Forest for the Trees: Social Networks and the Prediction of Romantic Relationship State and Fate." *Journal of Personality and Social Psychology* 81, no. 6 (2001): 1042.

Allport, Gordon W. *Pattern and Growth in Personality.* New York: Harcourt, 1963.

Bouchard, Thomas J. Jr., and Matt McGue. "Genetic and Environmental Influences on Human Psychological Differences." *Journal of Neurobiology* 54, no. 1 (2003): 4–45.

Bradbury, Thomas N., Frank D. Fincham, and Steven R. H. Beach. "Research on the Nature and Determinants of Marital Satisfaction: A Decade in Review." *Journal of Marriage and Family* 62, no. 4 (2004): 964–80.

Burt, S. Alexandra. "Genes and Popularity Evidence of an Evocative Gene-Environment Correlation." *Psychological Science* 19, no. 2 (2008): 112–13.

Caspi, Avshalom, Alan Taylor, Terrie E. Moffitt, and Robert Plomin. "Neighborhood Deprivation Affects Children's Mental Health: Environmental Risks Identified in a Genetic Design." *Psychological Science* 11, no. 4 (2000): 338–42.

Caughlin, John P., Ted L. Huston, and Renate M. Houts. "How Does Personality Matter in Marriage? An Examination of Trait Anxiety, Interpersonal Negativity, and Marital Satisfaction." *Journal of Personality and Social Psychology* 78, no. 2 (2000): 326.

Costa, Paul T., Jr., Jeffrey H. Herbst, Robert R. McCrae, and Ilene C. Siegler. "Personality at Midlife: Stability, Intrinsic Maturation, and Response to Life Events." *Assessment* 7, no. 4 (2000): 365–78.

Dawes, Robyn M., David Faust, and Paul E. Meehl. "Clinical Versus Actuarial Judgment." *Science* 243, no. 4899 (1989): 1668–74.

Fowers, Blaine J., Eileen Lyons, Kelly H. Montel, and Netta Shaked. "Positive Illusions about Marriage among Married and Single Individuals." *Journal of Family Psychology* 15, no. 1 (2001): 95.

Gottman, John M., and Robert W. Levenson. "Marital Processes Predictive of Later Dissolution: Behavior, Physiology, and Health." *Journal of Personality and Social Psychology* 63, no. 2 (1992): 221.

Grove, William M., David H. Zald, Boyd S. Lebow, Beth E. Snitz, and Chad Nelson. "Clinical Versus Mechanical Prediction: A Meta-Analysis." *Psychological Assessment* 12, no. 1 (2000): 19.

Heine, Steven J., and Emma E. Buchtel. "Personality: The Universal and the Culturally Specific." *Annual Review of Psychology* 60 (2009): 369–94.

Kelley, Harold H., John G. Holmes, Norbert L. Kerr, Harry T. Reis, Caryl E. Rusbult, and Paul A. M. Van Lange. *An Atlas of Interpersonal Situations.* Cambridge: Cambridge University Press, 2003.

Lucas, Richard E. "Adaptation and the Set-Point Model of Subjective Well-Being: Does Happiness Change After Major Life Events?" *Current Directions in Psychological Science* 16, no. 2 (2007): 75–79.

Meehl, Paul E. *Clinical Versus Statistical Prediction: A Theoretical Analysis and a Review of the Evidence.* Minneapolis: University of Minnesota Press, 1954.

Ozer, Daniel J., and Veronica Benet-Martinez. "Personality and the Prediction of Consequential Outcomes." *Annual Review of Psychology* 57 (2006): 401–21.

Plomin, Robert, and John Crabbe. "DNA." *Psychological Bulletin* 126, no. 6 (2000): 806.

Roberts, Brent W., Avshalom Caspi, and Terrie E. Moffitt. "The Kids Are Alright: Growth and Stability in Personality Development from Adolescence to Adulthood." *Journal of Personality and Social Psychology* 81, no. 4 (2001): 670.

Rutter, Michael, and Judy Silberg. "Gene-Environment Interplay in Relation to Emotional and Behavioral Disturbance." *Annual Review of Psychology* 53, no. 1 (2002): 463–90.

Sroufe, L. Alan, Byron Egeland, Elizabeth Carlson, and W. Andrew Collins. "Placing Early Attachment Experiences in Developmental Context: The Minnesota Longitudinal Study." in *Attachment from Infancy to Adulthood: The Major Longitudinal Studies,* New York: Guilford Press, 2005.

Turkheimer, Eric, and Mary Waldron. "Nonshared Environment: A Theoretical, Methodological, and Quantitative Review." *Psychological Bulletin* 126, no. 1 (2000): 78.

Waldinger, Robert J., Marc S. Schulz, Stuart T. Hauser, Joseph P. Allen, and Judith A. Crowell. "Reading Others' Emotions: The Role of Intuitive Judgments in Predicting Marital Satisfaction, Quality, and Stability." *Journal of Family Psychology* 18, no. 1 (2004): 58.

Westen, Drew, and Joel Weinberger. "When Clinical Description Becomes Statistical Prediction." *American Psychologist* 59, no. 7 (2004): 595.

CHAPTER 7

Botwin, Michael D., David M. Buss, and Todd K. Shackelford. "Personality and Mate Preferences: Five Factors in Mate Selection and Marital Satisfaction." *Journal of Personality* 65, no. 1 (2006): 107–36.

Connelly, Brian S., and Deniz S. Ones. "An Other Perspective on Personality: Meta-Analytic Integration of Observers' Accuracy and Predictive Validity." *Psychological Bulletin* 136, no. 6 (2010): 1092.

Dyrenforth, Portia S., Deborah A. Kashy, M. Brent Donnellan, and Richard E. Lucas. "Predicting Relationship and Life Satisfaction from Personality in Nationally Representative Samples from Three Countries: The Relative Importance of Actor, Partner, and Similarity Effects." *Journal of Personality and Social Psychology* 99, no. 4 (2010): 690.

Funder, David C. "Personality." *Annual Review Of Psychology* 52 (2001), 197–221.

Funder, David C. "Towards a Resolution of the Personality Triad: Persons, Situations, and Behaviors." *Journal of Research in Personality* 40, no. 1 (2006): 21–34.

Funder, David C., R. Michael Furr, and C. Randall Colvin. "The Riverside Behavioral Q-Sort: A Tool for the Description of Social Behavior." *Journal of Personality* 68, no. 3 (2008): 451–89.

Funder, David C., and Stephen G. West. "Consensus, Self-Other Agreement, and Accuracy in Personality Judgment: An Introduction." *Journal of Personality* 61, no. 4 (2006): 457–76.

Gagné, Faby M., and John E. Lydon. "Bias and Accuracy in Close Relationships: An Integrative Review." *Personality and Social Psychology Review* 8, no. 4 (2004): 322–38.

Gosling, Samuel D., Peter J. Rentfrow, and William B. Swann. "A Very Brief Measure of the Big-Five Personality Domains." *Journal of Research in Personality* 37, no. 6 (2003): 504–28.

Johnson, Wendy, Matt McGue, Robert F. Krueger, and Thomas J. Bouchard Jr. "Marriage and Personality: A Genetic Analysis." *Journal of Personality and Social Psychology* 86, no. 2 (2004): 285.

Jonason, Peter K., Norman P. Li, and David M. Buss. "The Costs and Benefits of the Dark Triad: Implications for Mate Poaching and Mate Retention Tactics." *Personality and Individual Differences* 48, no. 4 (2010): 373–78.

Malouff, John M., Einar B. Thorsteinsson, Nicola S. Schutte, Navjot Bhullar, and Sally E. Rooke. "The Five-Factor Model of Personality and Relationship Satisfaction of Intimate Partners: A Meta-Analysis." *Journal of Research in Personality* 44, no. 1 (2010): 124–27.

Markon, Kristian E., Robert F. Krueger, Thomas J. Bouchard, and Irving I. Gottesman. "Normal and Abnormal Personality Traits: Evidence for Genetic and Environmental Relationships in the Minnesota Study of Twins Reared Apart." *Journal of Personality* 70, no. 5 (2002): 661–94.

McCrae, Robert R., Paul T. Costa Jr., Fritz Ostendorf, Alois Angleitner, Martina Hřebíčková, Maria D. Avia, Jesús Sanz, Maria L. Sánchez-Bernardos, M. Ersin Kusdil, Ruth Woodfield, Peter R. Saunders, and Peter B. Smith. "Nature over Nurture: Temperament, Personality, and Life Span Development." *Journal of Personality and Social Psychology* 78, no. 1 (2000): 173.

Robins, Richard W., Avshalom Caspi, and Terrie E. Moffitt. "Two Personalities, One Relationship: Both Partners' Personality Traits Shape the Quality of Their Relationship." *Journal of Personality and Social Psychology* 79, no. 2 (2000): 251.

Watson, David, and Lee Anna Clark. "On Traits and Temperament: General and Specific Factors of Emotional Experience and Their Relation to the Five-Factor Model." *Journal of Personality* 60, no. 2 (2006): 441–76.

Watson, David, Brock Hubbard, and David Wiese. "General Traits of Personality and Affectivity as Predictors of Satisfaction in Intimate Relationships: Evidence from Self- and Partner-Ratings." *Journal of Personality* 68, no. 3 (2000): 413–49.

Watson, David, Brock Hubbard, and David Wiese. "Self–Other Agreement in Personality and Affectivity: The Role of Acquaintanceship, Trait Visibility, and Assumed Similarity." *Journal of Personality and Social Psychology* 78, no. 3 (2000): 546.

Witt, Edward A., and M. Brent Donnellan. "Furthering the Case for the MPQ-Based Measures of Psychopathy." *Personality and Individual Differences* 45, no. 3 (2008): 219–25.

CHAPTER 8

Bowlby, John. *A Secure Base.* New York: Routledge, 2005.

Cassidy, Jude. "Adult Romantic Attachments: A Developmental Perspective on Individual Differences." *Review of General Psychology* 4, no. 2 (2000): 111.

Cassidy, Jude, and Phillip Shaver, eds. *Handbook of Attachment: Theory, Research, and Clinical Applications.* New York: Guilford Press, 2008.

Ceglian, Cindi Penor, and Scott Gardner. "Attachment Style: A Risk for Multiple Marriages?" *Journal of Divorce & Remarriage* 31, no. 1–2, (1999): 125–39.

Collins, Nancy L., and Brooke C. Feeney. "A Safe Haven: An Attachment Theory Perspective on Support Seeking and Caregiving in Intimate Relationships." *Journal of Personality and Social Psychology* 78, no. 6 (2000): 1053.

Fraley, R. Chris, and Phillip R. Shaver. "Adult Romantic Attachment: Theoretical Developments, Emerging Controversies, and Unanswered Questions." *Review of General Psychology* 4, no. 2 (2000): 132.

Fraley, R. Chris, and Phillip R. Shaver. "Airport Separations: A Naturalistic Study of Adult Attachment Dynamics in Separating Couples." *Journal of Personality and Social Psychology* 75, no. 5 (1998): 1198.

Fraley, R. Chris, Amanda M. Vicary, Claudia Chloe Brumbaugh, and Glenn I. Roisman. "Patterns of Stability in Adult Attachment: An Empirical Test of Two Models of Continuity and Change." *Journal of Personality and Social Psychology* 101, no. 5 (2011): 974.

Frazier, Patricia A., Anne L. Byer, Ann R. Fischer, Deborah M. Wright, and Kurt A. DeBord. "Adult Attachment Style and Partner Choice: Correlational and Experimental Findings." *Personal Relationships* 3, no. 2 (2005): 117–36.

Hazan, Cindy, and Phillip Shaver. "Romantic Love Conceptualized as an Attachment Process." *Journal of Personality and Social Psychology* 52, no. 3 (1987): 511.

Johnson, Susan M., and Paul S. Greenman. "The Path to a Secure Bond: Emotionally Focused Couple Therapy." *Journal of Clinical Psychology* 62, no. 5 (2006): 597–609.

Kertes, Darlene A., Megan R. Gunnar, Nicole J. Madsen, and Jeffrey D. Long. "Early Deprivation and Home Basal Cortisol Levels: A Study of Internationally Adopted Children." *Development and Psychopathology* 20, no. 2 (2008): 473.

Klohnen, Eva C., and Stephan Bera. "Behavioral and Experiential Patterns of Avoidantly and Securely Attached Women across Adulthood: A 31-Year Longitudinal Perspective." *Journal of Personality and Social Psychology* 74, no. 1 (1998): 211.

Li, Tianyuan, and Darius K. S. Chan. "How Anxious and Avoidant Attachment Affect Romantic Relationship Quality Differently: A Meta-Analytic Review." *European Journal of Social Psychology* 42, no. 4 (2012): 406–19.

Main, Mary, and Judith Solomon. "Procedures for Identifying Infants as Disorganized/Disoriented during the Ainsworth Strange Situation." *Attachment in the Preschool Years: Theory, Research, and Intervention* 1 (1990): 121–60.

McWilliams, Lachlan A., and S. Jeffrey Bailey. "Associations between Adult Attachment Ratings and Health Conditions: Evidence from the National Comorbidity Survey Replication." *Health Psychology* 29, no. 4 (2010): 446.

Roisman, Glenn I., Elena Padrón, L. Alan Sroufe, and Byron Egeland. "Earned–Secure Attachment Status in Retrospect and Prospect." *Child Development* 73, no. 4 (2003): 1204–19.

Suomi, Stephen J., Mary L. Collins, Harry F. Harlow, and Gerald C. Ruppenthal. "Effects of Maternal and Peer Separations on Young Monkeys." *Journal of Child Psychology and Psychiatry* 17, no. 2 (2006): 101–12.

Weinfield, Nancy S., L. Alan Sroufe, and Byron Egeland. "Attachment from Infancy to Early Adulthood in a High-Risk Sample: Continuity, Discontinuity, and Their Correlates." *Child Development* 71, no. 3 (2000): 695–702.

CHAPTER 9

Acevedo, Bianca P., Arthur Aron, Helen E. Fisher, and Lucy L. Brown. "Neural Correlates of Marital Satisfaction and Well-Being: Reward, Empathy, and Affect." *Clinical Neuropsychiatry* 9 (2012): 20–31.

Berns, Sara B., Neil S. Jacobson, and John M. Gottman. "Demand-Withdraw Interaction in Couples with a Violent Husband." *Journal of Consulting and Clinical Psychology* 67, no. 5 (1999): 666.

Berscheid, Ellen. "The Greening of Relationship Science." *American Psychologist* 54, no. 4 (1999): 260.

Bradbury, Thomas N., and Frank D. Fincham. "Attributions and Behavior in Marital Interaction." *Journal of Personality and Social Psychology* 63, no. 4 (1992): 613.

Bradbury, Thomas N., and Frank D. Fincham. "Attributions in Marriage: Review and Critique." *Psychological Bulletin* 107, no. 1 (1990): 3.

Caughlin, John P. "The Demand/Withdraw Pattern of Communication as a Predictor of Marital Satisfaction over Time." *Human Communication Research* 28, no. 1 (2002): 49–85.

Christensen, Andrew, and Christopher L. Heavey. "Gender and Social Structure in the Demand/Withdraw Pattern of Marital Conflict." *Journal of Personality and Social Psychology* 59, no. 1 (1990): 73.

Gable, Shelly L., Courtney L. Gosnell, Natalya C. Maisel, and Amy Strachman. "Safely Testing the Alarm: Close Others' Responses to Personal Positive Events." *Journal of Personality and Social Psychology* 103, no. 6 (2012): 963–81.

Gable, Shelly L., and Harry T. Reis. "Good News! Capitalizing on Positive Events in an Interpersonal Context." *Advances in Experimental Social Psychology* 42 (2010): 195–257.

Gable, Shelly L., Harry T. Reis, Emily A. Impett, and Evan R. Asher. "What Do You Do When Things Go Right? The Intrapersonal and Interpersonal Benefits of Sharing Positive Events." *Journal of Personality and Social Psychology* 87, no. 2 (2004): 228.

Gottman, John M., and Robert W. Levenson. "Marital Processes Predictive of Later Dissolution: Behavior, Physiology, and Health." *Journal of Personality and Social Psychology* 63, no. 2 (1992): 221.

Gottman, John M., and Robert W. Levenson. "The Timing of Divorce: Predicting When a Couple Will Divorce over a 14-Year Period." *Journal of Marriage and Family* 62, no. 3 (2004): 737–45.

Karney, Benjamin R., and Thomas N. Bradbury. "Attributions in Marriage: State or Trait? A Growth Curve Analysis." *Journal of Personality and Social Psychology* 78, no. 2 (2000): 295.

Karney, Benjamin R., Thomas N. Bradbury, Frank D. Fincham, and Kieran T. Sullivan. "The Role of Negative Affectivity in the Association between Attributions and Marital Satisfaction." *Journal of Personality and Social Psychology* 66, no. 2 (1994): 413.

MacGregor, Jennifer C. D., and John G. Holmes. "Rain on My Parade: Perceiving Low Self-Esteem in Close Others Hinders Positive Self-Disclosure." *Social Psychological and Personality Science* 2, no. 5 (2011): 523–30.

CHAPTER 10

Caughlin, John P., and Anita L. Vangelisti. "An Individual Difference Explanation of Why Married Couples Engage in the Demand/Withdraw Pattern of Conflict." *Journal of Social and Personal Relationships* 17, no. 4–5 (2000): 523–51.

Christensen, Andrew, and Neil S. Jacobson. *Reconcilable Differences.* New York: Guilford Press, 2002.

Christensen, Andrew, and Neil S. Jacobson. "Who (or What) Can Do Psychotherapy: The Status and Challenge of Nonprofessional Therapies." *Psychological Science* 5, no. 1 (1994): 8–14.

Folkman, Susan, Richard S. Lazarus, Rand J. Gruen, and Anita DeLongis. "Appraisal, Coping, Health Status, and Psychological Symptoms." *Journal of Personality and Social Psychology* 50, no. 3 (1986): 571.

Haverkamp, Beth E., and Ty D. Tashiro. "Cognitive Structures and Motives as Barriers to Insight: Contributions From Social Cognition Research." Chap. 17 in *Insight in Psychotherapy.* Washington, D.C.: American Psychological Association, 2007.

Helson, Ravenna, and Brent W. Roberts. "Ego Development and Personality Change in Adulthood." *Journal of Personality and Social Psychology* 66, no. 5 (1994): 911.

Hopko, Derek R., C. W. Lejuez, and Sandra D. Hopko. "Behavioral Activation as an Intervention for Coexistent Depressive and Anxiety Symptoms." *Clinical Case Studies* 3, no. 1 (2004): 37–48.

Karney, Benjamin R., Thomas N. Bradbury, Frank D. Fincham, and Kieran T. Sullivan. "The Role of Negative Affectivity in the Association between Attributions and Marital Satisfaction." *Journal of Personality and Social Psychology* 66, no. 2 (1994): 413.

Lejuez, Carl W., Derek R. Hopko, James P. LePage, Sandra D. Hopko, and Daniel W. McNeil. "A Brief Behavioral Activation Treatment for Depression." *Cognitive and Behavioral Practice* 8, no. 2 (2001): 164–75.

Lyubomirsky, Sonja. *The How of Happiness: A Scientific Approach to Getting the Life You Want.* New York: Penguin, 2008.

Noftle, Erik E., and Phillip R. Shaver. "Attachment Dimensions and the Big Five Personality Traits: Associations and Comparative Ability to Predict Relationship Quality." *Journal of Research in Personality* 40, no. 2 (2006): 179–208.

Norcross, John C., Paul M. Krebs, and James O. Prochaska. "Stages of Change." *Journal of Clinical Psychology* 67, no. 2 (2011): 143–54.

Propp, Vladimir. *Morphology of the Folktale*. Translated by Laurence Scott. Austin: University of Texas Press, 1971.

Roberts, Brent W., Kate E. Walton, and Wolfgang Viechtbauer. "Patterns of Mean-Level Change in Personality Traits across the Life Course: A Meta-Analysis of Longitudinal Studies." *Psychological Bulletin* 132, no. 1 (2006): 1.

Seligman, Martin E. P., and Mihaly Csikszentmihalyi. "Positive Psychology: An Introduction." *American Psychologist* 55, no. 1 (2000): 5.

Shryack, Jessica, Michael F. Steger, Robert F. Krueger, and Christopher S. Kallie. "The Structure of Virtue: An Empirical Investigation of the Dimensionality of the Virtues in Action Inventory of Strengths." *Personality and Individual Differences* 48, no. 6 (2010): 714–19.

Spencer, Amy. *Meeting Your Half-Orange: An Utterly Upbeat Guide to Using Dating Optimism to Find Your Perfect Match*. Philadelphia: Running Press, 2010.

Tashiro, Ty, and Patricia Frazier. "The Causal Effects of Emotion on Couples' Cognition and Behavior." *Journal of Counseling Psychology* 54, no. 4 (2007): 409.

ACKNOWLEDGMENTS

I am grateful to many talented and kind people. Laurie Abkemeier has been unbelievably supportive, deeply insightful and, in general, more than one could wish for in an agent. My editor, Deb Brody, provided a wonderful combination of sage advice and bright enthusiasm, which has given me confidence to explore and grow.

Numbers cannot quantify and words cannot express my gratitude to my family, including my parents, Trae, Tia, Jamie, Jeff, Kim, Brooke and many others.

My friends have provided much needed expertise and levity, including Andie, Kelly, Amy, Kiley, Jeff, Sarah, Carl, Sara, Lisa, Lorilee and Robyn. I am forever grateful to Pat, who spent countless hours teaching me to think clearly and write with purpose, and to Ellen, who introduced me to the potential of relationship science. A special thanks for Ashley, who provided creative energy and unwavering faith in me.

I know that it is highly improbable to be surrounded by so many remarkable people who possess so many wonderful characteristics, which is exactly why I feel so lucky in my interpersonal life.

INDEX